C000143666

1,000,000 Books

are available to read at

Forgotten Books

---◆---

www.ForgottenBooks.com

---◆---

Read online
Download PDF
Purchase in print

ISBN 978-1-5282-0475-0
PIBN 10917312

This book is a reproduction of an important historical work. Forgotten Books uses
state-of-the-art technology to digitally reconstruct the work, preserving the original format
whilst repairing imperfections present in the aged copy. In rare cases, an imperfection in
the original, such as a blemish or missing page, may be replicated in our edition. We do,
however, repair the vast majority of imperfections successfully; any imperfections that
remain are intentionally left to preserve the state of such historical works.

Forgotten Books is a registered trademark of FB &c Ltd.
Copyright © 2018 FB &c Ltd.
FB &c Ltd, Dalton House, 60 Windsor Avenue, London, SW19 2RR.
Company number 08720141. Registered in England and Wales.

For support please visit www.forgottenbooks.com

1 MONTH OF
FREE
READING

at

www.ForgottenBooks.com

By purchasing this book you are eligible for one month membership to ForgottenBooks.com, giving you unlimited access to our entire collection of over 1,000,000 titles via our web site and mobile apps.

To claim your free month visit:
www.forgottenbooks.com/free917312

* Offer is valid for 45 days from date of purchase. Terms and conditions apply.

English
Français
Deutsche
Italiano
Español
Português

www.forgottenbooks.com

Mythology Photography **Fiction**
Fishing Christianity **Art** Cooking
Essays Buddhism Freemasonry
Medicine **Biology** Music **Ancient
Egypt** Evolution Carpentry Physics
Dance Geology **Mathematics** Fitness
Shakespeare **Folklore** Yoga Marketing
Confidence Immortality Biographies
Poetry **Psychology** Witchcraft
Electronics Chemistry History **Law**
Accounting **Philosophy** Anthropology
Alchemy Drama Quantum Mechanics
Atheism Sexual Health **Ancient History**
Entrepreneurship Languages Sport
Paleontology Needlework Islam
Metaphysics Investment Archaeology
Parenting Statistics Criminology
Motivational

The Private Collection of A Connoisseur

BRUSSELS RENAISSANCE & PARIS XVII CENTURY
TAPESTRIES ∾ BROCADES AND VELVETS

BLUE-AND-WHITE & DECORATED PORCELAINS
SEMI-PRECIOUS MINERAL CARVINGS

Sold By Order of the Owner
Mr. Edson Bradley
NEW YORK & NEWPORT

Under Management of the
American Art Association
INCORPORATED
New York
1927

Priced Catalogues

Priced copies of the catalogue, or any session thereof, will be furnished by the Association at charges commensurate with the duties involved in copying the necessary information from the records of the Association.

The AMERICAN ART ASSOCIATION · Inc

Designs its Catalogues
and Directs All Details of Illustration
Text and Typography

1. REJECTION OF BIDS. Any bid which is not commensurate with the value of the article offered, or which is merely a nominal or fractional advance, may be rejected by the auctioneer if in his judgment such bid would be likely to affect the sale injuriously.

2. THE BUYER. The highest bidder shall be the buyer, and if any dispute arises between two or more bidders, the auctioneer shall either decide the same or put up for re-sale the lot so in dispute.

3. IDENTIFICATION AND DEPOSIT BY BUYER. The name of the buyer of each lot shall be given immediately on the sale thereof, and when so required, each buyer shall sign a card giving the lot number, amount for which sold, and his or her name and address. ⅭⅬ A deposit at the actual time of the sale shall be made of all or such part of the purchase prices as may be required. ⅭⅬ If the two foregoing conditions are not complied with, the lot or lots so purchased may at the option of the auctioneer be put up again and re-sold.

4. RISK AFTER PURCHASE. Title passes upon the fall of the auctioneer's hammer, and thereafter the property is at the purchaser's risk, and neither the consignor nor the Association is responsible for the loss of, or any damage to any article by theft, fire, breakage, however occasioned, or any other cause whatsoever.

5. DELIVERY OF PURCHASES. Delivery of any purchases will be made only upon payment of the total amount due for all purchases at the sale.

6. RECEIPTED BILLS. Goods will only be delivered on presentation of a receipted bill. A receipted bill presented by any person will be recognized and honored as an order by the buyer, directing the delivery to the bearer of the goods described thereon. If a receipted bill is lost before delivery of the property has been taken, the buyer should immediately notify the Association of such loss.

7. STORAGE IN DEFAULT OF PROMPT PAYMENT AND CALLING FOR GOODS. Articles not paid for in full and not called for by the purchaser or agent by noon of the day following that of the sale may be turned over by the Association to some carter to be carried to and stored in some warehouse until the time of the delivery therefrom to the purchaser, and the cost of such cartage and storage and any other charges will be charged against the purchaser and the risk of loss or damage occasioned by such removal or storage will be upon the purchaser. ⅭⅬ In any instance where the purchase bill has not been paid in full by noon of the day following that of the sale, the Association and the auctioneer reserve the right, any other stipulation in these conditions of sale notwithstanding, in respect to any or all lots included in the purchase bill, at its or his option, either to cancel the sale thereof or to re-sell the same at public or private sale without further notice for the account of the buyer and to hold the buyer responsible for any deficiency and all losses and expenses sustained in so doing.

8. SHIPPING. Shipping, boxing or wrapping of purchases is a business in which the Association is in no wise engaged, but the Association will, however,

afford to purchasers every facility for employing at current and reasonable rates carriers and packers; *doing so*, however, without any assumption of responsibility on its part for the acts and charges of the parties engaged for such service.

9. GUARANTY. The Association exercises great care to catalogue every lot correctly and endeavors therein and also at the actual time of the sale to point out any error, defect or imperfection, but guaranty is not made either by the owner or the Association of the correctness of the description, genuineness, authenticity or condition of any lot and no sale will be set aside on account of any incorrectness, error of cataloguing or imperfection not noted or pointed out. Every lot is sold "as is" and without recourse. ⊄ Every lot is on public exhibition one or more days prior to its sale, and the Association will give consideration to the opinion of any trustworthy expert to the effect that any lot has been incorrectly catalogued and in its judgment may thereafter sell the lot as catalogued or make mention of the opinion of such expert, who thereby will become responsible for such damage as might result were his opinion without foundation.

10. RECORDS. The records of the auctioneer and the Association are in all cases to be considered final and the highest bid shall in all cases be accepted by both buyer and seller as the value against which all claims for losses or damage shall lie.

11. BUYING ON ORDER. Buying or bidding by the Association for responsible parties on orders transmitted to it by mail, telegraph, or telephone, if conditions permit, will be faithfully attended to without charge of commission. Any purchases so made will be subject to the foregoing conditions of sale, except that, in the event of a purchase of a lot of one or more books by or for a purchaser who has not through himself or his agent been present at the exhibition or sale, the Association will permit such lot to be returned within ten days from the date of sale, and the purchase money will be refunded, if the lot differs from its catalogue description. ⊄ Orders for execution by the Association should be given with such clearness as to leave no room for misunderstanding. Not only should the lot number be given, but also the title, and bids should be stated to be so much for the lot, and when the lot consists of one or more volumes of books or objects of art, the bid per volume or piece should also be stated. If the one transmitting the order is unknown to the Association, a deposit must be sent or reference submitted. Shipping directions should also be given.

These conditions of sale cannot be altered except by the auctioneer or by an officer of the Association

OTTO BERNET · HIRAM H. PARKE · *Auctioneers*

AMERICAN ART ASSOCIATION · INC

Managers

CATALOGUE

FOREWORD

THE outstanding achievements of textile craft in the fifteenth and sixteenth centuries are the magnificent velvets woven on the looms of Genoa and Venice, the skilful and meticulous ecclesiastical embroideries of England, Spain and Italy, and the master-tapestries of the Late Gothic and the Renaissance periods, which reached their apex in the products of the Brussels *ateliers*. This transition period was marked everywhere by an earnest devotion to detail; not with the spirit of a decadence, but rather with the joyful care taken by the discoverers of a treasure, in counting their guineas. The amazing wealth of ornament invented or unearthed by the artists of the time is incredible enough to an age infertile in such art-forms; but it is the collector himself who marvels, *more suo*, at the endless diversification of the fabrics of his collections. No elaborate critical vocabulary can obscure the essential rightness, the good taste, of these masterpieces of design.

Further, to such beauty as that of the Gothic *ferronnerie* velvets, age has added the quality of patina; in this respect the superb cut velvet cope [No. 328] with its orphreys of *opus anglicanum*, is one of the most beautiful vestments outside the Wardrobe of the Vatican. In a brief survey of the collection, it is impossible to do more than mention the sumptuous array of a dozen or more embroidered copes; the crimson and ruby Genoese velvets of the XVI-XVII centuries, of which Mr. Bradley has assembled some scores of varieties, many of large size; the Portuguese gold-embroidered velvets from the great Benguiat collection of 1919; the crimson damasks and brocatelles of Italy in Baroque compositions of heroic size; the brocades, needlepainted orphreys and the considerable assortment of eighteenth century tassels, which, in common with most antique *passementerie*, are now virtually unprocurable.

Two important tapestry series belonging to Mr. Edson

Bradley will be on exhibition; the Louis XIV *History of Dido and Aeneas*, and the three Brussels Renaissance hangings depicting *The Story of Samson*, signed by the master Jan Raes, who flourished in Antwerp and Brussels during the years 1620-30.

In addition to the fabrics a number of Chinese mineral carvings and porcelains will be offered. The former include a few fine jades of the reign of *Ch'ien-lung*, the latter a group of vases of the *lang yao* family, an unusually large and beautiful piece of steatitic ["soft paste"] porcelain, examples of *Chün* and *Ting* ware and *famille rose* types of the eighteenth and nineteenth centuries.

L. A. H.

FIRST SESSION
Friday November 11, 1927 at 2:15 p.m.
Catalogue Numbers 1 to 185A Inclusive

1. ONYX AGATE PATCH BOX

Oblong, with chamfered corners. Of rich tortoiseshell agate.

Length, 2¾ inches

2. AGATE PATCH BOX

Of smoky agate, with gilded mounts. Opens in two sections.

Length, 3 inches

3. CARVED AND GILDED HAUT-RELIEF VOTIVE PLAQUE

Italian School

MADONNA AND CHILD. Half-length figure of the hooded Madonna holding on her right arm the Child, who is supported by a cherub-head.

Height, 11½ inches; width, 9 inches

4. LIMOGES ENAMEL PLAQUE

By Couly le Nouailler II, XVI Century

Figure of a nun in robes of brown and cobalt-blue, kneeling in prayer, against a green background. Brown floral border. Framed.

Height, 5½ inches; width, 4¼ inches

5. LIMOGES ENAMEL PLAQUE *French, Late XVI Century*

Figure of our Lord of the Resurrection, wrapped in a reddish-brown cloak and carrying a banner; on either side are the prostrate figures of Roman soldiers. Background of mountainous landscape. Framed.

Length, 7¾ inches; width, 6 inches

6. ANTIQUE TORTOISESHELL COFFRET INLAID WITH SILVER

Oblong, with segmental top. Veneered in rich dark tortoise-shell, with floral rosettes and spandrels of silver.

Length, 8 inches

7. SATSUMA GLOBULAR JAR AND KYOTO FLAMBÉ SWEETMEAT BOX

[A] Grayish stonelike ware with fleckings resembling the tea-dust effect.

[B] Flat circular box with *jaspé* blue and brown markings.

Height of (a) 9 inches
Diameter of (b) 6 inches

8. COFFRET IN SIXTEENTH CENTURY MOSS-GREEN VELVET

Of wood; with gilded iron lock, clasps and bands.

Length, 9½ inches

9. TWO ARMORIAL CHAMPLEVÉ ENAMEL BOOK COVERS
French, Early XVII Century

Border in cobalt-blue reserved in copper, with scrolls of leaves through which are leaping four white hounds; central plaquette with a floral device and an escutcheon bearing an eagle in a white field.

Length of each, 11 inches; width, 8¾ inches

10. RHAGES IRIDESCENT PITCHER   *Persian, XII Century*

Pear-shaped body with loop handle and spout. Copper-green glaze with rich iridescence.

Height, 5 inches

11. DERUTA MAJOLICA LUSTRE PLATE
Italian, Early XVI Century

Centre with quatrefoil ornament, marly with a border of spikes and floral ornament sketched in underglaze cobalt and enriched with yellow lustre. [Much repaired.]

Diameter, 8½ inches

16

12. RHAGES COPPER-GREEN IRIDESCENT PLATE
Persian, circa XII Century
Deep plate with flat marly; grayish-ivory body coated with a brilliant copper-green glaze with gorgeous rainbow iridescence.
Diameter, 10¼ *inches*

13. ENGRAVED IVORY POWDER HORN   *German Baroque*
Enriched with classical scenes beneath canopies, with bands of leafage. Brown patina.
Length, 10¼ *inches*

14. TWO BASKETWARE SALT GLAZE PLATES
English, XVIII Century
Finely molded with rococo latticed and valanced rims, with pierced basketware design and checkered centres. [Repaired.]
Diameters, 9 *inches and* 10½ *inches*

15. THREE TERRA-COTTA GROUPS   *Tanagra Style*
Seated figure of a young woman; two bibulous figures of old men; one of whom has fallen in the act of drinking; and a young woman seated on the back of an equine monster. [Needs slight repair.]
Heights, 7, 9 *and* 6½ *inches*

16. BRONZE ANIMAL STATUETTE   *Signed, Barye*
Muscular figure of a lion passant, oblong base. Cast by F. Barbedienne. Green patina.
Length, 16½ *inches*
[Companion to the following]

17. BRONZE ANIMAL STATUETTE   *Signed, Barye*
Vigorous figure of a lioness passant, on oblong base. Cast by F. Barbedienne.
Length, 16½ *inches*
[Companion to the preceding]

18. PAIR LOUIS XVI CUIVRE DORÉ WALL ORNAMENTS

In the form of tasseled drapery pendants crested by bow-knotted ribbons.

Length, 21 *inches*

19. RENAISSANCE CARVED AND GILDED RELIQUARY FRAME

Oval vitrine, the back in sixteenth century moss-green velvet; supported by two putti bearing scrolled branches crested with a coronet.

Height, 31½ *inches*

SEMI-PRECIOUS MINERAL CARVINGS

20. JAPANESE AMBER MANJU-NETSUKE

Huge circular button finely carved with the figure of the god Kinko riding on the back of a carp amid the waves. Unusually large specimen.

Diameter, 3½ *inches*

21. TWO CARVED MUTTON-FAT JADE MEDALLIONS

Each oval and pierced with floral scrollings amid which are writhing figures of monsters.

Diameter of each, 3½ *inches*

22. CARVED WHITE JADE BUCKLE

In the form of two rings pierced and carved as birds and monsters, and joined by an engraved link.

23. CARVED AMBER GROUP

Seated figure of the god of Contentment beneath a pine tree, beside a huge wine jar; on the reverse a fawn, beneath pine trees. Rich ruddy amber. Has stand.

Height, 3½ *inches*

24. CARVED ROCK CRYSTAL COVERED VASE

Pear-shaped vase mounted on the back of a swimming duck; oval cover with kylin finial. Has stand.

Height, 5 inches

25. CARVED MUTTON-FAT JADE PLAQUE, OR MIRROR HOLDER

Elaborately pierced with clouds, among which is the writhing body of the fierce dragon, clasping the flaming ball.

Diameter, 6½ inches

26. CARVED ROCK CRYSTAL VASE

In the form of a hollow tree-trunk encircled by branches bearing citrons and peaches, at which birds are pecking. Has stand.

Height, 6 inches

27. CARVED JADE LOTUS VASE

Tall vase in the form of a cup sheathed in leaves; of greenish mutton-fat jade. Has stand.

Height, 6½ inches

28. CARVED ROCK CRYSTAL INCENSE BURNER, WITH COVER

Cauldron-shaped, with kylin-head ring handles and three stump feet. Cover with kylin finial. Has stand.

Height, 4 inches

29. CARVED AMETHYSTINE QUARTZ COVERED VASE

Ch'ien-lung

In the shape of a double gourd hollowed and fitted with cover, meshed in branches bearing leaves and smaller gourds.

Height, 6 inches

30. CARVED JADE VASE   *K'ang-hsi*

In the form of a hollowed trunk wreathed with branches of pine trees, amid which are two cranes. Has stand.

Height, 6 inches

Charles Waggaman Collection, American Art Association,
1905

31. IMPERIAL CARVED YELLOW JADE TWIN VASE

Ch'ien-lung

In the form of a flattened pear-shaped vase with cover, adjoining a hollowed trunk; the two linked by the branches of pine and hawthorn trees, above which are flying bats, emblems of Happiness. Has stand.

Height, 7½ inches

[Illustrated]

32. CARVED JADE DOUBLE LOTUS VASE   *Ch'ien-lung*

Beautifully conceived in the form of a trailing branch with a blossom and two large lotus buds, hollowed out and fitted with covers, on one of which is a mantis. Greenish-gray softly polished jade. Has carved stand.

Length, 12 inches

[Illustrated]

33. CARVED SPINACH JADE BOWL   *Ch'ien-lung*

Circular, with two finely carved butterfly ring handles and six short feet. Interior carved with water plants and fungus, the exterior finely chiseled with reeds and lotus plants, amid which are flying birds. Deep spinach-green jade with black mottlings. Has carved stand. [One foot slightly damaged.]

Diameter, 13 inches

[Illustrated]

No. 31. Imperial Carved
Yellow Jade Twin Vase

No. 33. Carved Spinach Jade
Bowl

No. 32. Carved Jade Double Lotus Vase

34. CLOISONNÉ ENAMEL INCENSE BURNER   *Ming*

Oblong, with two S-curved lug handles; four stump feet ornamented with masks. Decoration of the Eight Buddhist Symbols amid lotus scrollings in a turquoise-blue ground. Teakwood base and cover with carnelian agate finial.

Height, 9 *inches*

35. CLOISONNÉ ENAMEL INCENSE BURNER   *K'ang-hsi*

Decoration of lotus palmettes and chrysanthemums amid leaves and scrolling tendrils in a turquoise-blue ground; three stump feet. [Rim and handles of later date.]

Diameter, 5½ *inches*

PASSEMENTERIE, DAMASKS, BROCADES
BROCATELLES AND VELVETS

36. SET OF FOUR YELLOW SILK AND GOLD TASSELS

Latticed body and gold thread skirts of yellow silk and gold.

37. TWO PAIRS ASSORTED ROSE-CRIMSON SILK TASSELS

XVIII Century

One in rose-pink and white, with looped cords; the other in crimson and gold with pompon skirts and long cords.

38. THREE PAIRS ASSORTED SILK TASSELS

Louis XIV and Louis XV Periods

Comprising a pair in emerald-green and white, a pair in tan and white, and a pair in tan, terra-cotta, and écru.

39. SIX PAIRS ASSORTED SILK TASSELS   *XVIII Century*

Comprising a pair in blue and white silk, a pair in tan, two pairs in golden-yellow, a pair in crimson, and a pair in white and gold.

40. FOUR PAIRS ASSORTED SILK TASSELS

French, XVIII Century

Comprising a pair in salmon-pink and yellow, a pair of finger tassels in blue and yellow, a pair in yellow and gold, and a pair in sapphire-blue, white and yellow.

41. SIX PAIRS ASSORTED SILK TASSELS   *XVIII Century*

Comprising a pair in crimson and gold, a pair in rose and blue, two pairs in yellow and gold, a pair in pale orange, and a pair in blue and white.

42. SET OF SIX GOLD AND YELLOW SILK TASSELS

Louis XVI Period

With silk double cords, latticed heads, and fringed skirts.

43. EIGHT ASSORTED SILK TASSELS   *XVIII Century*

A pair in écru and gold, two pairs in yellow and gold, and a pair in white and tan.

44. LOT OF ASSORTED PASSEMENTERIE

Comprising two seventeenth century crimson silk tassels, a crimson silk tassel, a blue silk tassel, a crimson tassel, and a strip of gold fringe with spiral tassels and pendants.

45. EMBROIDERED GOLDEN-YELLOW SATIN STRIP AND
    SIXTEENTH CENTURY VELVET BOURSE

[A] Strip of satin beautifully embroidered in brilliant silks with serpentine scrolling branches of tulips, peonies, and other blossoms and leafage, of the early eighteenth century. [B] Genoese crimson velvet embroidered in silver with *fleur-de-lys* ornament.

23

46. GOLD, SILVER AND SILVER-EMBROIDERED VOTIVE
APPLIQUÉ   *French, Louis XIV Period*
Beautifully worked with a border of leafy branches supporting shell motives and enclosing a silver monstrance sustained on three cherub-heads and flanked by leaping putto
holding wheat-ears and grapes, symbolic of the harvest.

47. FIVE GOLD AND SILK-EMBROIDERED ESCUTCHEONS
Spanish and Italian, XVI-XVIII Century
Various; including a pair of coroneted Spanish escutcheons,
two *cardinalizio* escutcheons and one coroneted gold escutcheon.

48. TWO GOLD AND SILK-EMBROIDERED ESCUTCHEONS
Coroneted; one quartered with drap d'argent and orange velvet, the other restored.

49. SIX GOLD, SILVER AND SILK-EMBROIDERED ESCUTCHEONS
Italian, XVI-XVII Century
Including a pair of escutcheons of a bishop with green hat
and pendent *fiocci;* two archepiscopal escutcheons with pendent *fiocci;* and two coroneted escutcheons, one with the in-
signia of the Order of St. Francis.

50. SEVEN ASSORTED AMICES
Including a pair in seventeenth century emerald silk damask,
a pair in Spanish Louis XVI floral brocade, a pair in sixteenth
century embroidered velvet and a silver and silk-embroidered
amice of the Louis XIV period.

51. TWO PAIRS EMBROIDERED ECCLESIASTICAL ESCUTCHEONS
Italian, XVII Century
One with elaborately scrolled yellow shield surmounted by
the crozier and red hat of an archbishop, with pendent *fiocci;*
the other with a gold and silver shield with green hat and
fiocci.

52. ANTIQUE NEEDLEPOINT BELL PULL

Petit point ground worked in *gros point* with scrolling branches enriched with leaves and tiny roses and enclosing fantastic figures of winged male and female centaurs, the faces enriched with silk.

Length, 5 feet 7 inches

53. LENGTH OF ANTIQUE CHINESE CRIMSON SATIN BROCADE BORDER

Rose-crimson ground developing a running design of serpentine scrollings and branches of formalized lotus blossoms, between narrower borders of similar design. Six pieces. [Slightly discolored in parts.]

Length, 13 yards; width, 10 inches

54. PAIR GOLD-EMBROIDERED DRAP D'ARGENT STOLES

Italian, XVII Century

White silk ground woven with silver threads and beautifully embroidered in gold with a running motive of scrolling leafy branches supporting fruit, amid which are figures of birds; the ends display strap scrollings supported by a shield motive and centring a floral cross.

Length, 6 feet 6 inches

55. PAIR LARGE SILVER-EMBROIDERED ESCUTCHEONS

Spanish, XVII Century

Elaborate baroque leaf-scrolled mantling centring an oval cartouche charged with a bridge and three towers. In heavily padded silver threads.

56. TWO EMERALD-GREEN SILK DAMASK STOLES AND THREE MANIPLES *Italian, Louis XIII Period*

Design of short scrolling stems bearing tulips and pomegranates, etc., supported on curving branches.

Length of stoles, 6 feet 10 inches

57. APPLIQUÉ EMBROIDERED ARMORIAL VELVET PANEL

Of deep green eighteenth century velvet, enriched with a seventeenth century quartered escutcheon surmounted by a coronet and mantled with leafy branches.

58. VALANCE AND SMALL TABLE RUNNER OF JARDINIÈRE
VELVET   *Genoese, XVII Century*

[A] Symmetrical floral designs in a pinkish ivory ground; [B] Floral motives in claret, salmon-pink and leaf-green, with borders of emerald-green velvet.

59. SET OF GOLD-EMBROIDERED PURPLE VELVET SADDLE
TRAPPINGS   *Italian, XVIII Century*

Composed of three pieces; richly embroidered in padded gold threads and tinsel with borders of interlacing rococo ribbon motives enriched with leafage.

60. SILK-EMBROIDERED ECCLESIASTICAL BANNER AND VELVET
TABLE COVER

[A] Swallow-tailed Jesuit banner embroidered in colored silks with upstanding bouquet of flowers, birds, and butterflies enclosing a figure of the Paschal Lamb on a missal; of Chinese workmanship.

[B] Table cover of eighteenth century green velvet with an oval panel of Louis XIV jardinière velvet.

61. PAIR GOLD- AND SILVER-EMBROIDERED GENOESE VELVET
BORDERS   *Italian, XVI Century*

Beautifully worked in gold and silver threads and blue, green and yellow silks with a symmetrical Renaissance design of interlacing leaf-scrolled strapwork supporting tulips and other blossoms and baskets of leafage, and emitting delicate tendrils.

Length, 4 feet 5 inches; width, 9 inches

26

62. TWO GREEN CUT VELVET CUSHION COVERS

Italian, XVII Century

Bold symmetrical Louis XIV floral designs *à deux hauteurs* in a satin ground of lighter tone.

63. PAIR WINE-RED VELVET TABLE COVERS

Genoese, Early XVII Century

Brilliant fluctuating silk velvet with rose sheen; bordered and cross-banded with gold galloon.

Length, 4 feet 6 inches; width, 9 feet 3 inches

64. THREE VALANCE POINTS OF DRAP D'OR APPLIQUÉ CRIMSON SILK EMBROIDERY   *Portuguese, XVII Century*

Patterned with symmetrical skeletonized floral devices in crimson silk *appliqué* on a cloth-of-gold ground.

Depth, 1 foot 10 inches

65. MOSS-GREEN CUT VELVET PANEL   *Louis XIV Period*

Developing, on a canary-colored ground, a bold symmetrical pattern of huge scrolling branches of curling leafage, supporting a species of scaly fruit from which grows a blossom.

Length, 58 inches; width, 51 inches

66. GENOESE GARNET VELVET VALANCE

Trimmed with gold galloon and finished with silk ball fringe. Lined.

Length, 5 feet 1 inch; depth, 15 inches

67. SET OF JARDINIÈRE VELVET CHAIR COVERS

Genoese, XVII Century

Comprising two backs and two seats. Symmetrical floral design *à deux hauteurs* in purple, crimson, aquamarine, fawn and green, in a tan ground. [Worn.]

68. Appliqué Embroidered Ruby Velvet Border
Florentine, XVI Century

Worked in colored silks outlined with *cordonnets* in a design of swirling yellow leafage supporting convolvulus, honeysuckle and other blossoms, with delicate floral borders.

Length, 10 feet; depth, 1 foot 3 inches

69. Ruby Velvet Table Cover   *Genoese, XVII Century*

Lustrous shimmering velvet of fluctuating tone; banded in gold galloon.

Length, 7 feet; width, 6 feet 9 inches

70. Embroidered Botticelli-green and Rose-crimson Velvet Chasuble   *Italian, XVI-XVII Century*

Of lustrous rose velvet with old patina; orphrey of green velvet embroidered in gold thread and colored silks with scrolling trails of blossoms and leafage.

[Illustrated]

71. Rose-red Cut Velvet Panel   *Louis XIV Period*

Large symmetrical pattern of broad scrolling frames enriched with leafage and enclosing heavy bunches of flowers and foliage, woven *à deux hauteurs* against a ground of lighter tone.

Length, 5 feet 5 inches; width, 4 feet

72. Embroidered Genoese Crimson Velvet Valance
Italian, XVI Century

Comprising two pieces totaling six points. Old velvet enriched with running cusped ornament in broad gold galloon, trimmed with gold fringe.

Total length, 12 feet; depth, 2 feet 2 inches

No. 70. Embroidered Botticelli-green and Rose-crimson Velvet Chasuble

73. GOLD- AND SILK-EMBROIDERED IVORY SATIN CHASUBLE
Italian, XVIII Century

Worked with a glittering design in gold thread of interlacing branches and ribbons; with borders of wheatears and supporting beautifully embroidered roses, carnations, tulips, cornflowers and other blossoms, and bunches of grapes.

[Illustrated]

74. GENOESE GARNET VELVET VALANCE

Three pieces. Dark velvet with amber lights, trimmed with gold galloon and fringe.

Total length, 19 feet 3 inches; depth, 18 inches

75. GOLD, SILVER- AND SILK-EMBROIDERED VELVET PANEL
Persian, XVII Century

Of crimson velvet, embroidered with a stellate rosette enclosed within incurved branches bearing angularly scrolling twigs with blossoms and a serpentine floral border. In padded gold and silver threads, centred with colored silks.

76. TWO FIGURED VELVET TABLE COVERS
Chinese, XVIII-XIX Century

One of green velvet patterned with interlacing scrolling branches supporting curved leaves and fantastic human figures; the other of deep green patterned with intertwining scrollings of leaves.

Length of one, 52 inches; width, 48 inches
Length of one, 43 inches; width, 19 inches

77. GOLD BROCADE CHASUBLE   *Italian, Late XVII Century*

Ivory ground enriched in gold thread, rose, wine-red, orange and yellow silks with descending trails of blossoms and leafage interrupted by balustrades and rococo portals.

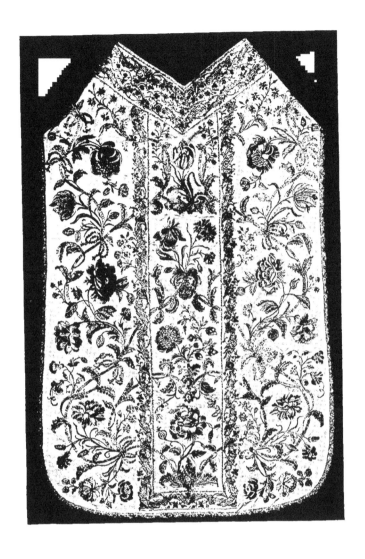

No. 73. Gold- and Silver-embroidered Ivory Satin Chasuble

78. TWO PANELS OF DRAP D'OR CUT VELVET

Russian, XVIII Century

Primrose-yellow ground enriched with gold threads and woven with a Louis XV design in amber velvet of parallel serpentine branches of blossoms.

79. APPLIQUÉ EMBROIDERED MOSS-GREEN VELVET BORDER

Italian, XVI Century

Developing in *appliqué* yellow silk outlined with white *cordonnets* a symmetrical Renaissance design of ogivals of ribbon enclosing single leaves and emitting scrollings of leaves.

Length, 4 feet 11 inches; width, 7½ inches

80. JADE-GREEN CUT VELVET PANEL   *Italian, XVII Century*

Symmetrical Louis XIV floral design, boldly scrolled, in a pinkish-tan ground. Bordered with sixteenth century deep emerald-green velvet.

Length, 54 inches; width, 26 inches

81. NEEDLEPAINTED RUBY VELVET ECCLESIASTICAL BANNER

Spanish, XVI-XVII Century

Swallow-tail banner of metallic ruby-red with soft lustre; embroidered with an oval garland of roses enclosing a large standing figure of the Virgin of the Crescent and the Child, within a glory.

Length, 5 feet 7 inches; width, 3 feet 2 inches

[Illustrated]

82. STRIPED GOLDEN-YELLOW SATIN LAMPAS HANGING

Italian, Early XVIII Century

Brilliant satin ground, woven in sage and olive-green with a bold design of a serpentine branch bearing leaves, tendrils and berries and contained between lilac and yellow stripes.

Length, 7 feet 6 inches; width, 6 feet 8 inches

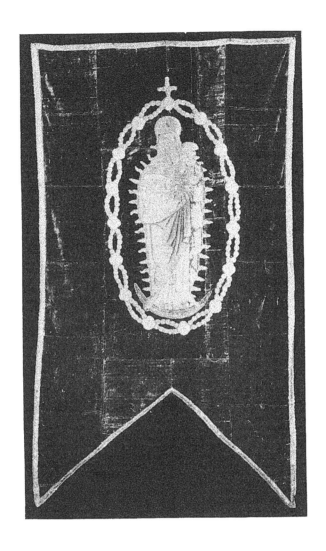

No. 81. Needlepainted Ruby Velvet Ecclesiastical Banner

83. Two Strips of Renaissance Rose-crimson Silk Damask

Italian, circa 1600

Patterned with double ogivals of ribbon interlinked by coronets and enclosing scrolled spade-shaped leafage devices. [Repaired.] *Length,* 16 *feet* 3 *inches; width,* 21½ *inches*

84. Armorial Crimson Silk Damask Hanging

Italian, Late XVII or Early XVIII Century

Design of leaf-scrolled frames linked by coronets and enclosing successively a coroneted eagle; a lion rampant bearing a banderolle with a motto: OMNIBUS IDEM, surmounting a shield barry, and a cartouche charged with a tree on a mountain of six summits.

Length, 9 *feet* 5 *inches; width,* 7 *feet* 11 *inches*

85. Emerald-green Silk Damask Panel   *Spanish Rococo*

Allover Régence design of symmetrical spade-shaped nosegays of flowers and leafage.

Length, 6 *feet* 6 *inches; width,* 3 *feet* 7 *inches*

86. Chinese Crimson and White Satin Brocade Panel

Rose-crimson satin ground developing an allover pattern of scrolling gold peonies and camellias. [Stained.]

Length, 6 *feet* 4 *inches; width,* 4 *feet* 8 *inches*

87. Taupe Cut Velvet and Embroidery Chasuble

Spanish, XVI-XVII Century

Orphreys of rare sapphire-blue velvet *appliqués* in yellow satin outlined in gold thread and enriched with colored silks, with a symmetrical Renaissance design of vases and interlacing leaf scrollings with tendrils, and a panel portraying the Virgin of the Crescent and the Child. Field of seventeenth century taupe cut velvet with a gray ground and design of scrolling branches of blossoms.

[Illustrated]

34

No. 87. Taupe Cut Velvet and Renaissance Embroidery Chasuble

88. SHELL-PINK SATIN BROCADE PANEL   *Spanish, circa* 1700

Developing in green and ivory, broad spade-shaped frame-works of leafage enclosed between serpentining scalloped ribbon branches and blossoms and supporting here and there clusters of tiny blue and yellow field flowers.

41 inches square

89. APPLIQUÉ EMBROIDERED CRIMSON SILK DAMASK VALANCE
Louis XIV Period

Rose-crimson floral damask scalloped and embellished with scrolled and leaf-enriched strap motives. Trimmed with silk fringe.

Length, 20 *feet* 2 *inches; depth,* 16 *inches*

90. SET OF FOUR SILVER-EMBROIDERED CRIMSON VELVET
SADDLE TRAPPINGS   *Spanish, Late XVII Century*

Comprising saddle cover and three housings, all of superb crimson velvet; the latter embroidered in silver thread enriched with sequins with interlacing and scrolling rococo branches supporting blossoms and centring coroneted escutcheons worked in gold, silver and silk threads, and charged per pale with a coroneted lion rampant, gules, and a field paly gules and or.

91. ROYAL JARDINIÈRE VELVET CHASUBLE
Genoese, XVII Century

Ivory ground, beautifully patterned *à deux hauteurs* with trailing masses of blossoms in Vandyke-brown, wine-red, rose and yellow, with rich dark green foliage.

[Illustrated]

No. 91. Royal Jardinière Velvet Chasuble

92. EMERALD-GREEN VELVET TABLE COVER
Spanish, XVII Century
Of variable tone, fluctuating from blue-green to a leaf-yellow, and bordered with gold galloon.

Length, 5 feet 5 inches; width, 3 feet 9 inches

93. LENGTH OF DRAP D'OR AND APPLIQUÉ VELVET
EMBROIDERED BORDER *Portuguese, circa* 1600
Yellow ground woven with gold threads and developing in *appliqué* crimson velvet a running pattern of interlacing voluted scrollings of leafage in the late Renaissance manner.

Total length, 16 feet; width, 10 inches

94. GOLD-WOVEN FLORAL BROCADE TABLE COVER
Chinese, XVIII Century
Patterned in oblongs of white and tawny-pink, and beautifully brocaded in gold and colored silks with rich interlacing branches of leafage and blossoms.

Length, 6 feet 7 inches; depth, 4 feet 4 inches

95. PAIR LOUIS TREIZE CRIMSON SILK DAMASK HANGINGS
Italian, Early XVII Century
Symmetrical design of pairs of vigorously curving leafy branches linked by coronets and enclosing jardinières of roses, tulips and other blossoms. Trimmed with gold galloon.

Length, 8 feet 6 inches; width, 3 feet 7 inches

96. LOUIS TREIZE CRIMSON SILK DAMASK HANGING
Italian, Early XVII Century
Similar to the preceding, but differing in size.

Length, 7 feet 11 inches; width, 5 feet 1 inch

38

97. FILET LACE TABLE CLOTH AND RUNNER, AND
     EMBROIDERED LINEN COVER

Spanish, XVII-XVIII Century

Geometrical stellate design and borders of serpentine leafage ornament; the cover embroidered with three scrolled rosettes and voluted lattice borders in tan and blue.

Lengths, 8 feet 10 inches; 4 feet 8 inches; 7 feet 4 inches

98. FOUR LINEN AND FIL TIRÉ TABLE RUNNERS

Spanish, XVII-XVIII Century

Geometrical design of stellate figures and latchhooked diamond figures, varied by vases of carnations.

Lengths, 7 feet; 6 feet 7 inches; 6 feet 6 inches; 6 feet 2 inches

99. TWO LENGTHS OF ROSE-CRIMSON SILK DAMASK

Italian, Louis XIII Period

Patterned with ribbon ogivals looped with coronets and enclosing scrolled spatulate foliage devices. [One faded.]

Total length, 17 feet 4 inches; widths, 1 foot 8 inches and 1 foot 10 inches

100. LEAF-GREEN AND GOLDEN-YELLOW BROCATELLE CHASUBLE

Italian Renaissance

Ground of primrose-yellow, woven with ogivals of ivory enclosing spade-shaped floral devices and interlacing with scrolling green branches; with orphreys of old-gold and pale green fabric developing symmetrical leaf scrolls and branches of pomegranates.

101. ROSE-CRIMSON VELVET VALANCE   *Genoese, XVII Century*

Superb velvet with heavy pile and rose sheen. Scalloped and ornamented with gold galloon and fringe.

Length, 10 feet; depth, 2 feet

102. FOUR LENGTHS OF ASSORTED CRIMSON AND ROSE-PINK SILK
DAMASK   *Louis XIII Period*

Baroque design of short scrolling stems of tulips and leafage swaying in alternate directions.

Lengths, 8 feet 10 inches; 8 feet 8 inches; 7 feet 6 inches; 6 feet 8 inches

103. GENOESE JARDINIÈRE VELVET PANEL
Italian, XVII Century

Developing on an ivory ground huge symmetrical sprays of flowers and leafage beneath latticed canopies of leaves and blossoms, in orange, mulberry, sky-blue, yellow and emerald.

Length, 37 inches; width, 45 inches

104. TWO LENGTHS OF CRIMSON SILK DAMASK
Italian, XVII Century

Gigantic design of huge blossoms with stems of curving pointed leaves, and curling branches of pendent pomegranates.

Total length, 12 yards 1 foot; width, 1 foot 6 inches

105. RUBY VELVET TABLE COVER   *Genoese, XVII Century*

Four widths of deep and brilliant ruby velvet with soft patina; border in gold galloon.

7 feet square

106. FOUR FRAGMENTS OF CRIMSON AND YELLOW SILK
BROCATELLE   *Italian, XVII Century*

Cloth of old-gold and crimson, patterned in rose-crimson with a bold symmetrical motive of huge intersecting branches of scrolling foliage centring a spray of leaves upon which stands the figure of the Pilgrim, St. Roch, with his staff and dog. [One piece worn.]

Length, 8 yards 6 inches; width, 2 feet

107. PRIMROSE-YELLOW SILK DAMASK TABLE COVER

Régence Period

Symmetrical design of spade-shaped floral sprays supported
on either side by nosegays of blossoms and leafage.

Length, 5 feet 9 inches; width, 4 feet 4 inches

108. FOUR DRAP D'OR CRIMSON CUT VELVET PANELS

Italian, Early XVIII Century

Softly glittering ground woven with broad opposed latticed
ribbons serpentining and enriched with floral trails, and enclosing a symmetrical floral spray.

Length of two, 6 feet 10 inches; width, 10 inches
Length of two, 47 inches; width, 10 inches

*Vitall and Leopold Benguiat Collection, American Art Asso-
ciation, 1919*

109. PAIR GOLD-WOVEN IVORY SILK DAMASK VALANCES

Louis XIV Period

Symmetrical design *damassé* and brocaded in gold, of spatulate bouquets of flowers enclosed by floral arches. Trimmed
with gold galloon and fringed. In all, six points.

Total length, 12 feet 6 inches; depth, 28 inches

110. RENAISSANCE BROCATELLE TABLE COVER

Spanish, Early XVI Century

Golden-yellow ground patterned in ivory with leaf ogivals
interlacing with scrolling crimson branches, and supporting
and enclosing Gothic pomegranate figures surrounded by
ivory leafage. A rare piece, of unusual size.

Length, 7 feet; width, 6 feet 5 inches

41

111. THREE CRIMSON SILK DAMASK HANGINGS
Italian Baroque

Symmetrical design of scrolling floral branches forming ogivals and enclosing huge sprays of leafage and flowers. Each one two widths.

Total length, 16 yards 2 feet; width, 1 foot 9 inches

112. EMBROIDERED GARNET VELVET VALANCE
Genoese, Late XVI or Early XVII Century

Valance or refectory table runner of dark rich velvet, embellished with three *appliqués* of strap arabesques and bordered with gold galloon and fringe.

Length, 15 feet 4 inches; width, 24 inches

113. APPLIQUÉ EMBROIDERED CRIMSON SILK DAMASK VALANCE
Italian, XVII Century

Louis XIV damask enriched with leafage and strapwork *appliqués* in yellow satin. Fringed.

Length, 9 feet 10½ inches; depth, 13 inches

114. PAIR SMALL GENOESE CRIMSON VELVET WINDOW HANGINGS
Italian, XVII Century

Soft velvet with fluctuating rose tones. Bordered with gold galloon.

Length of each hanging, 7 feet 2 inches; width, 23 inches

115. LOUIS XIV CRIMSON AND IVORY CUT VELVET COPE
Genoese, XVII Century

Ivory satin ground with a bold design in deep crimson *à deux hauteurs* of latticed jardinières supporting pomegranates and floral sprays within frames of symmetrical scrolling leafage. With hood.

Length, 9 feet 5 inches; depth, 4 feet 6 inches
[Illustrated]

42

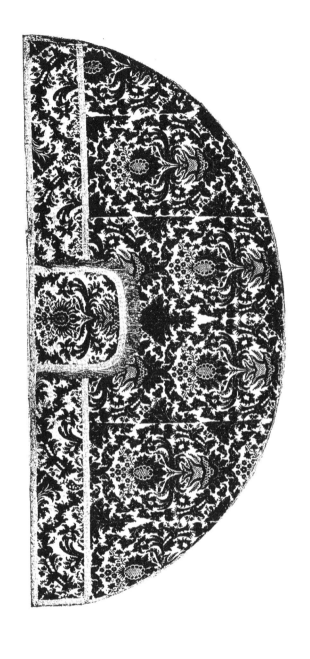

No. 115. Louis XIV Crimson and Ivory Cut Velvet Cope

116. PAIR APPLIQUÉ SILK-EMBROIDERED WINE-RED VELVET
BORDERS *Florentine, XVI Century*

Worked in *appliqué* painted silks outlined with *cordonnets* in
a continuous symmetrical design of pairs of opposed interlacing scrollings of leafage enriched with tendrils and supporting floral motives, with delicate running borders of tiny
trefoils. *Length, 8 feet 9 inches; width, 9½ inches*

117. LOUIS XIV JARDINIÈRE VELVET PANEL
Genoese, Late XVII Century

Graceful symmetrical design *à deux hauteurs,* on cream
ground, of trophies of foliage enclosed by scrolling leafy
branches and blossoms, and woven in claret, shell-pink,
fawn and shades of emerald and cypress-green.

Length, 5 feet 8 inches; width, 22 inches

118. DEEP CRIMSON VELVET TABLE COVER
Spanish, XVII Century

Soft and brilliant fabric with thick pile, and dark, almost
black tones; bordered with gold galloon.

Length, 8 feet 8 inches; width, 6 feet

119. LOUIS QUATORZE CRIMSON AND IVORY CUT VELVET
VALANCE *Genoese, XVII Century*

Striking symmetrical design of large masses of scrolling foliage supporting pomegranates and pairs of curving fuchsias
and other blossoms. Trimmed with silver fringe.

Length, 6 feet 8 inches; depth, 15 inches

120. EMERALD-GREEN VELVET AND SILK DAMASK DORSAL
Italian, XVI-XVII Century

Of superb sixteenth century Genoese velvet with soft yellow lights; banded with Louis Treize green damask enriched
with three *appliqués* stellate figures of crimson silk.

Length, 6 feet 9 inches; width, 3 feet

44

121. THREE EMBROIDERED ROSE-CRIMSON VELVET VALANCES
                                    Genoese, XVI Century
Rich velvet, with patina of age.   Enriched with *appliqué*
cusped and scrolled strapwork ornament in gold galloon,
trimmed with gold fringe.   Various.

> *Length of one, 5 feet; depth, 18 inches*
> *Length of one, 3 feet 10 inches; depth, 21 inches*
> *Length of one, 4 feet; depth, 24 inches*

122. EMERALD-GREEN SILK BROCADE TABLE COVER
                                    Louis XIV Period
Brilliantly woven in blues, reds, fawn, deep green, purple
and silver with gnarled branches bearing at intervals superb
sprays of roses, cornflowers, pinks and other blossoms, and
lightly shaded fawn leafage.

> *Length, 53 inches; width, 46 inches*

123. RARE RENAISSANCE DRAP D'OR CRIMSON CUT VELVET
      PANEL   *Venetian, XVI Century*
Mellow golden ground patterned in raised crimson pile with
a diamond lattice of tiny leaf sprays enclosing small bunches
of roses, each with three blossoms.

> *Length, 62 inches; width, 51 inches*

124. BOTTICELLI-GREEN VELVET AND EMERALD SILK DAMASK
      CHASUBLE   *Spanish Renaissance*
Damask patterned with ogivals of ribbons interlinked by
coronets and enclosing spade-shaped scrolled leaf motives;
orphreys of sixteenth century green velvet.

45

125. EMBROIDERED CRIMSON CUT VELVET VALANCE

Portuguese, XVII Century

Comprising three pieces totaling nine points. Ground of Louis XIV cut velvet with *appliqué* in an elaborate symmetrical design of scrolled and cusped strapwork supporting sprays of leaves. Trimmed with gold galloon and fringe.

Length, 5 yards 8 inches; depth, 2 feet 10 inches

126. EMBROIDERED COPE AND TWO DALMATICS

Spanish, Late XVI Century

Of heavy white rep, embroidered in laid *cordonnets* with orphreys bearing a symmetrical Renaissance design of opposed scrolling branches supporting various blossoms, together with borders of blue and tan leaf scrollings; and *semé* with scattered scrolled floral stems.

Length of cope, 9 feet 11 inches; depth, 5 feet

127. RENAISSANCE GOLD- AND SILVER-EMBROIDERED RUBY
VELVET CANTONNIÈRE   *Italian, XVI Century*

Of dark crimson Genoese velvet superbly worked in gold and silver thread and *appliqués* silks with a symmetrical running design of leaf scrollings supporting tulips and delicate tendrils interrupted by vases of fruit and terminating in chimera heads, with delicate borders of latticed strapwork.

Length, 7 feet 7 inches; depth of side pieces, 2 feet 3 inches; width, 11 inches

[Illustrated]

128. CRIMSON SILK DAMASK COVERLET   *Louis XIV Period*

Graceful symmetrical design of large nosegays enclosed within scrolled frames of flowers and leafage supporting pairs of cornucopiae filled with blossoms.

Length, 8 feet 7 inches; width, 8 feet

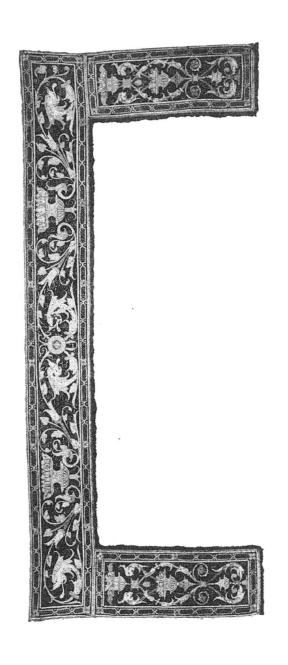

No. 127. Renaissance Gold- and Silver-embroidered Ruby Velvet
Cantonnière

129. TWO APPLIQUÉS EMBROIDERED CRIMSON VELVET COLUMN
HANGINGS   *Spanish, Early XVII Century*
Design worked in laid floss silks outlined with *cordonnets* on
appliqués of cloth-of-gold, outlined with laid tapes. Developing huge scrolled and cusped frames of acanthus leafage and flowers, enclosing blossoms and *corbeilles,* and supporting a pair of *adossés* figures of exotic parrots.

Length, 9 feet 6 inches; width, 19 inches

130. EMERALD-GREEN SILK DAMASK COPE *Louis XIII Period*
Symmetrical design of rows of small bouquets of leafage
and pairs of pendent tulips, supported on a *dentelé* framework; bordered with narrow braid. Has hood.

Length, 9 feet 6 inches; depth, 4 feet 6 inches

131. PAIR EMERALD-GREEN SILK DAMASK DALMATICS
Louis XIII Period
To match the preceding.

132. EMERALD-GREEN SILK DAMASK CHASUBLE
Louis XIII Period
To match the preceding.

133. WINE-RED FIGURED VELVET TABLE COVER
Italian, Late XVI Century
Soft rich fabric of brilliant wine-crimson, *frappé* with an
allover design of small interlacing C-scrolls enriched with
tendrils and interspersed with circular whorls. Trimmed
with broad gold and silver galloon.

Length, 6 feet 7 inches; width, 27 inches

134. CRIMSON VELVET VALANCE *Genoese, Late XVII Century*
Scalloped valance of rich crimson velvet with silky pile.
Eight points.

Length, 10 feet 8 inches; width, 20 inches

48

135. CHINESE SILK EMBROIDERED HANGING   *Ch'ien-lung*

Of black silk, beautifully embroidered in soft colors with large and small roundels filled with blossoms and utensils, with a narrow and a deep border of formalized rockery and waves bearing floating vases of flowers and Buddhistic emblems.

58 inches square

136. THREE LENGTHS OF CRIMSON VELVET

Italian, XVIII Century

Genoese velvet of varying tones and light weight. [Needs slight repair.]

Total length, 12 yards 6 inches; width, 19 inches

137. EMERALD-GREEN SATIN BROCADE DORSAL

Italian, circa 1700

Patterned with latticed fan-shaped floral devices enclosed by zigzag frames delicately enriched with blossoms and leafage.

Length, 5 feet 4 inches; width, 36 inches

138. LENGTH OF DRAP D'OR SILK APPLIQUÉ EMBROIDERED
     VALANCE   *Portuguese, XVII Century*

Comprising three strips of cloth of gold enriched with an *appliqué* of crimson silk of skeletonized sprays of leafage; trimmed with gold galloon and fringe.

Total length, 20 feet 6 inches; depth, 2 feet

Vitall and Leopold Benguiat Collection, American Art Association, 1919

139. PAIR APPLIQUÉ EMBROIDERED CRIMSON SILK DAMASK
HANGINGS   *Spanish, Louis XIV Period*

—Symmetrical design of huge sprays of flowers and leafage
supported on narrow ogivals of scrolling branches; enriched
with double borders in *appliqué* yellow silk embroidery of
interlacing leaf scroll design.

Length, 10 feet 3 inches; width, 2 feet 10 inches

140. PAIR POINT D'ARRAS SILK EMBROIDERY HANGINGS
Florentine, Early XVII Century

—Boldly worked in brilliant shaded silks with broad, scrolling
leafy branches bearing huge blossoms on which are perched
parrots, cockatoos and song birds; the silks laid in rows
of parallel threads in an ivory ground stitched with a lattice work. Trimmed with gold galloon and green silk fringe.

Length, 11 feet 5 inches; width, 3 feet 11 inches

*Vitall and Leopold Benguiat Collection, American Art Asso-
ciation, 1919*
[Illustrated]

141. EMBROIDERED GARNET VELVET REFECTORY TABLE RUNNER
Genoese, XVII Century

—Strip of sumptuous velvet in fine preservation, the ends enriched with *appliqué* embroidery of gold galloon in the form
of a looped and scrolled strapwork cartouche.

Length, 13 feet; width, 21 inches

142. CRIMSON VELVET BALDACCHINO
Genoese, XVII-XVIII Century

Brilliant silk velvet, centred with traces of a former *appliqué*
involving a flaming cross.

Length, 8 feet 3 inches; width, 9 feet 4 inches

No. 140. Pair Point d'Arras Silk Embroidery Hangings

143. ITALIAN RENAISSANCE LEAF-GREEN SILK DAMASK COPE
—Allover design of a pierced diamond lattice formed of links and enclosing ogival leaved pomegranate devices.

Length, 9 feet 10 inches; depth, 5 feet

144. PAIR GENOESE JARDINIÈRE VELVET HANGINGS
Louis XIV Period
Beautiful symmetrical design *à deux hauteurs* on a gray ground of ogival bouquets of blossoms and curving leafage in pastel reds, tans, yellows, sky-blue and olive-green.

Length, 6 feet 2 inches; width, 4 feet

[Illustrated]

145. APPLIQUÉ EMBROIDERED CRIMSON VELVET AND SILK
VALANCE   *Spanish, Late XVI Century*
Yellow silk ground *appliqué* in velvet outlined by *cordonnets* with a curious running design, developing a horizontal branch emitting fantastic gnarled twigs terminating in irregularly shaped leafage. Trimmed with deep yellow silk fringe.

Length, 22 feet 7 inches; depth, 9 inches

146. FOUR GENOESE RUBY VELVET VALANCES
Italian, XVI Century
Comprising three large valances, one of six, two of five panels, and one small valance of two panels, in heavy rich velvet bordered and banded with gold galloon. Trimmed with fringe.

Total length of three valances, 17 feet 6 inches; depth, 1 foot 5 inches
Length of small valance, 6 feet; depth, 10 inches

52

No. 144. Pair Genoese Jardinière Velvet Hangings

147. EMBROIDERED ROSE-CRIMSON VELVET BALDACCHINO

Genoese, Early XVII Century

A large and important canopy composed of six widths of sumptuous velvet enriched at the corners and the centres of the sides with an *appliqué* ornament of interlacing angular strap scrollings, of later date.

Length, 12 feet 9 inches; width, 9 feet 7 inches

148. CRIMSON VELVET AND APPLIQUÉ DRAP D'OR EMBROIDERED VALANCE *Portuguese, Early XVII Century*

Comprising three pieces, forming seven points. Of beautiful Genoese rose-crimson velvet *appliqué* in cloth-of-gold with symmetrical up-standing and scrolling sprays of six-petaled blossoms. Trimmed with gold galloon.

Length, 11 feet; depth, 2 feet 2 inches

149. TWO CRIMSON SILK DAMASK HANGINGS *Italian Baroque*

Developing an allover pattern of parallel serpentine ribbon motives interlacing with leaf scrolls and supporting rows of blossoms swaying in alternate directions.

Total length, 16 feet; width, 1 foot 9 inches

150. ECRU SATIN FLORAL BROCADE COPE

Italian, XVII Century

Richly woven with huge sprays of rose and salmon-pink blossoms with long fringed leaves, beneath branches of oak saplings with green and silvery leafage.

Length, 9 feet 2 inches; depth, 4 feet 5 inches

151. CRIMSON CUT VELVET AND APPLIQUÉ DRAP D'OR
　　EMBROIDERED VALANCE　　*Portuguese, XVII Century*
Of Louis XIV Genoese cut velvet with symmetrical design
overlaid by an *appliqué* of cloth-of-gold with an écru ground
developing large skeletonized sprays of leafage. Trimmed
with gold galloon and fringe. Four points.

Length, 8 feet; depth, 2 feet 6 inches

Vitall and Leopold Benguiat Collection, American Art Association, 1919

152. FRIEZE OF ROSE-CRIMSON AND YELLOW SILK BROCATELLE
　　　　　　　　　　　　Italian, XVII Century
Comprising four pieces. Recurring design of ogivals of
branches enclosing symmetrical spatulate nosegays of blossoms and leafage; narrow border above and below of scrolled
cardiform figures, the pattern in rose-crimson and old-gold.

*Total length, about 14 yards; depths, 2 feet 6 inches
and 2 feet 3 inches*

153. THREE CRIMSON SILK DAMASK COLUMN HANGINGS
　　　　　　　　　　　　Italian Baroque
Symmetrical design of enormous flowers supported on curving branches engaged at intervals by scrolling stems of huge
peonies.

Total length, 12 yards 1 inch; width, 3 feet

154. ROSE-CRIMSON SILK DAMASK HANGING
　　　　　　　　Spanish, Late XVII Century
Narrow design of huge symmetrical sprays of leafage supporting floral motives, between downpointed leaves and surmounted by pairs of spreading pomegranate blossoms.

Length, 8 feet 4 inches; width, 3 feet 5 inches

155. SILVER EMBROIDERY AND IVORY AND GOLD BROCADE COPE
Louis XV Period

—Of ivory silk brocaded in pastel shades of crimson, mauve and blue with serpentine scrolling green branches of flowers and golden fan-shaped leaves; the orphrey of blue silk damask, sumptuously embroidered in silk and silver threads with large scrolling leaves and wild roses, enriched with sequins.

Length, 9 feet; depth, 4 feet 3 inches

[Illustrated]

156. IVORY BAROQUE SILK BROCADE HANGING
Italian, circa 1700

Satin ground woven in ivory with a broad band of fan-shaped sprays of leaves supported on scrolled lattices and enriched with flowers picked out in blue, green and rose-pink, with serpentine trails of blossoms and leafage at either side. Four widths. [Needs slight repair.]

7 feet square

157. GENOESE CRIMSON VELVET AND BROCATELLE COPE
Italian, XVI Century

Rich deep crimson velvet of the late sixteenth or early seventeenth century with an orphrey of rare sixteenth century rose and golden-yellow Spanish brocatelle developing scrolled leaf ogivals enclosing Gothic leaved pomegranate devices.

Length, 9 feet 9 inches; depth, 4 feet 6 inches

Raoul Tolentino Collection, American Art Association, 1919

No. 155. Silver Embroidery and Ivory and Gold Brocade Cope

158. GENOESE CRIMSON VELVET AND RENAISSANCE GOLD
EMBROIDERY COPE   *Spanish, XVI Century*
Of beautiful deep velvet in superb preservation, with rose
patina; orphreys, hood and morse finely worked in gold with
a symmetrical embroidery of leaf-scrollings and tendrils with
pendent blossoms, and enclosed with six roundels, the hood
with a scrolled oval medallion in gold enclosing silk needlepainted figures of the Virgin of the Crescent and the Child
within a glory.

Length, 9 feet 2 inches; depth, 4 feet 7 inches

[Illustrated]

159. IMPORTANT RENAISSANCE RUBY VELVET PORTIÈRE
Genoese, XVI Century
Magnificent velvet with patinated areas showing interesting fluctuations in tone; mounted with broad gold galloon
and headed by a mock lambrequin with fringe.

Length, 11 feet 5 inches; width, 6 feet 5 inches

160. TWELVE LENGTHS OF ROSE-CRIMSON AND YELLOW SILK
BROCATELLE   *Lucca, Early XVII Century*
Developing an unusual design of small symmetrical spears
of leafage alternating with scrolling leaf ogivals centring
eight-pointed stars.

Total length, 34 yards 2 feet; width, 1 foot

No. 158. Genoese Crimson Velvet and Renaissance Gold Embroidery Cope

161. GOLD-EMBROIDERED RENAISSANCE RUBY VELVET HANGING
Italian, Late XVI Century

Magnificent heavy velvet with metallic patina and dark tones; worked in gold and silver threads with a border of leaf scrollings and floral trophies at the corners and centres of the sides, enclosing a scrolled circular cartouche containing a bunch of grapes and supporting Renaissance vases, embellished with delicate tendril motives.

Length, 6 feet 10 inches; width, 5 feet
[Illustrated]

162. AUBUSSON LOUIS SEIZE TAPESTRY CANTONNIÈRE

Graceful design, in the manner of the period, of bouquets of roses, asters, daisies and other garden flowers, supporting leaf scrollings festooned with delicate swags of roses. Mounted and trimmed with silk ball fringe.

Exterior height, 9 feet; width, 7 feet 5 inches
Interior height, 7 feet 9 inches; width, 5 feet

163. FLEMISH RENAISSANCE HUNTING TAPESTRY
Late XVI Century

LA CHASSE AUX ANIMAUX SAUVAGES. A meadow thickly wooded, with castle buildings and hills in the distance. A number of huntsmen with hounds are running about energetically and attacking a bear; in the foreground are a leopard, a bear, and dogs pursuing rabbits, in the left middle distance, a cavalier and a lady walking beside a lake beneath a grove of trees. Tan border woven in blues, greens, yellow and ivory with bunches of fruit and foliage, porticos and allegorical male and female figures including the figures of two monarchs playing on harps.

Height, 10 feet; length, 10 feet 10 inches

No. 161. Gold-embroidered Renaissance Ruby Velvet Hanging

164. PAIR ROYAL AUBUSSON TAPESTRY PANELS

Louis XVI Period

Vieil ivoire ground bordered with festoons of blossoms inter-twining with rose-pink ribbons and supporting a hanging bas-ket of flowers; at the centre of the base, a huge nosegay of roses, iris, phlox, poppies, and other garden flowers in nat-ralistic colors; the whole within an outer border of pale tur-quoise. Trimmed with silk fringe.

Length, 8 feet 3 inches; width, 7 feet 11 inches

[Illustrated]

165. PAIR LOUIS XIV ROYAL JARDINIÈRE VELVET HANGINGS

Ivory satin ground developing a flowing symmetrical design *à deux hauteurs* of sprays of blossoms in shaded mauves, tawny-reds and yellows, with pendent and scrolling olive-green leafage. Bordered with jardinière velvet braid.

Length, 7 feet 6 inches; width, 4 feet 1 inch

166. PAIR LOUIS XIV ROYAL JARDINIÈRE VELVET HANGINGS

Similar to the preceding, but deeper in tone.

Length, 7 feet 6 inches; width, 4 feet 1 inch

167. JADE-GREEN SILK DAMASK HANGING

Italian, XVII Century

Unusual symmetrical baroque design of frames of zigzag strapwork supporting pairs of conchiform vases and large clusters and branches of richly scrolling acanthus leaves.

Length, 9 feet 7 inches; width, 3 feet 10 inches

No. 164. Pair Royal Aubusson Tapestry Panels

168. IMPORTANT ROSE-CRIMSON VELVET PALACE BALDACCHINO

Genoese, Early XVII Century

In beautiful preservation, with the thick and soft pile of the sixteenth century velvets, and having two fluctuating bands of pale rose. Edging and double border of gold galloon.

Length, 14 feet 1 inch; width, 8 feet 9 inches

169. SET OF RUBY VELVET HANGINGS AND VALANCES

Genoese, XVII Century

Comprising two side curtains, long valance and two short valances. All of heavy lustrous velvet with wine-red tones, banded in gold galloon and trimmed with gold fringe.

Length of each side curtain, 8 feet 6 inches; width, 2 feet
Length of long valance, 7 feet 10 inches; depth, 18 inches
Length of two valances, 4 feet; depth, 12 inches

170. JAPANESE OR CHINESE AQUAMARINE SILK EMBROIDERED VALANCE

Of silk richly embroidered in brilliant colors with trees, flowers, and balustrades; the landscape filled with personages and children playing, carrying banners, canopies or utensils, blowing horns, or assisting at a procession figuring a huge sacred white elephant.

Length, 13 feet 6 inches; depth, 2 feet 2 inches

171. ROSE-CRIMSON VELVET BALDACCHINO

Genoese, XVI Century

Magnificent shimmering velvet with soft patina and fluctuating rose tones, bearing traces of former shell *appliqués* at the corners and two oval medallions at the centres of the sides. Banded with gold and silver galloon.

Length, 9 feet 10 inches; depth, 8 feet 9 inches

172. TWO SPANISH LOUIS XIV CRIMSON SILK DAMASK HANGINGS

Bold symmetrical design of huge sprays of flowers and leaf-age, surmounted by ogivals formed of pairs of curved and pointed leaves supporting pomegranates.

Length of one, 8 feet 2 inches; width, 3 feet 9 inches
Length of one, 7 feet 10 inches; width, 3 feet 9 inches

173. TWO SPANISH LOUIS XIV CRIMSON SILK DAMASK HANGINGS

Similar to the preceding.

Length, 8 feet 5 inches; width, 3 feet 9 inches

174. SET OF JADE-GREEN SILK DAMASK BED HANGINGS
Italian, Late XVII Century

Comprising tester cover, coverlet and three side hangings, the first two shaped and trimmed with silk ball fringe. Design of ogivals of strapwork enriched with leafage enclosing huge spatulate foliage ornaments.

175. LOUIS XIII GREEN AND YELLOW DAMASK COVERLET

Golden-yellow ground woven in deep emerald-green with rows of upstanding stems of flowers supported by pairs of small *adossés* figures of birds.

Length, 8 feet 8 inches; width, 7 feet 6 inches

176. SET OF CRIMSON SILK DAMASK HANGINGS
Italian, Late XVII Century

Comprising nine pieces. Mammoth symmetrical design of pairs of opposed scrolling branches sustaining leafage and pomegranates; a pair of curved and pointed leaves supports a missal surmounted by a flaming heart pierced by an arrow, above which floats a coronet with a pair of flying cherubs.

Total length, about 56 yards; widths from 30 to 39 inches

177. SUPERB JADE-GREEN VELVET BALDACCHINO

Genoese, XVII Century

Magnificent specimen of six widths of beautifully preserved velvet with long silken pile and fluctuating gray tones; bears traces of former *appliqués* of coroneted escutcheons and cartouches of interlacing scrolled strapwork at the corners and centres of the sides. Bordered in gold galloon.

Length, 13 feet 3 inches; width, 10 feet

[Illustrated]

178. SET OF FOUR ROSE-CRIMSON SILK DAMASK HANGINGS

Louis XIV Period

Gigantic design of leaf sprays forming huge ogivals supporting masses of foliage and pairs of pendent curved leaves and pomegranates. Of exceptional width.

Total length, 23 yards 30 inches; widths from 32½ inches to 39 inches

179. SET OF SPANISH LOUIS XIV CRIMSON SILK DAMASK ROOM HANGINGS

Comprising twenty-four pieces. Enormous symmetrical design of rich ogivals of leafage supporting huge floral bouquets with pairs of pendent curved leaves and pomegranates interspersed with blossoms.

Total length, about 102½ yards; width, 31 inches

180. GREEN AND YELLOW SATIN DAMASK COVERLET

Italian, XVII Century

Satin ground of old-gold, woven in pale green with a gigantic spray of flowers and leafage supported on an ogival formed of a pair of curved leaves, enclosing pomegranates and springing from masses of leafage below. Trimmed with silk fringe. [Slightly faded.]

Length, 8 feet; width, 9 feet

No. 177. Superb Jade-green Velvet Baldacchino

181. PAIR CRIMSON FIGURED VELVET HANGINGS

Centres of Régence velvet *frappé* with a symmetrical design of upstanding sprays of blossoms enclosed by ogivals and strapwork. Border developing close allover pattern of intertwined scrolled stems of tiny leaves. Banded in gold galloon; green silk damask lining.

Length of each, 10 feet 4 inches; width, 5 feet 5 inches

182. IVORY AND LEAF-GREEN SILK BROCATELLE HANGING
Italian, Louis XIII Period

Four widths. The design develops on a white ground a vase of tulips and carnations flanked by pairs of *adossés* birds and surrounded by clusters of large peonies and other flowers. Fringed.   *Length, 8 feet 9 inches; width, 7 feet*

183. PAIR ROSE-PINK SILK DAMASK PORTIÈRES

Of Louis XIV design, developing a large pattern of rococo leaf scrollings, symmetrically placed, and enriched with masses of flowers and foliage.

Length, 8 feet 1 inch; width, 4 feet 2 inches

A SUITE AND A PAIR OF CHAIRS

184. TWO MAHOGANY SIDE CHAIRS MOUNTED IN CUIVRE DORÉ
Second Empire Period

Square back and incurvate square legs. Crowning rail, splat and seat rail enriched with *appliqués* of putti dancing on floral swags, a beribboned Medusa head, leaf scrolls, etc. Seat in Empire crimson satin damask.

Two

185. SUITE OF ~~TEN~~ CARVED MAHOGANY SIDE CHAIRS

60.   *Chippendale Style*

Open fan-back enriched with leaf carving and interlacing
ribbon splat centred with husk motives. Leaf-carved cabri-
ole legs with ball-and-claw feet. Seats in green damask of
Renaissance design.

[One Illustrated]

69

185A. PALISSANDRE MARQUETERIE COMMODE

Italian, Late XVIII Century

Oblong top with quartered veneers and marqueterie of floral scrollings enclosing oval medallion; front with three drawers inlaid with ribbon borders, leaf scrollings, and medallion showing a seated figure of Aphrodite consigning a heart to the flames. Square tapering legs.

Height, 34½ inches; length, 50½ inches

[END OF FIRST SESSION]

SECOND AND LAST SESSION

Saturday November 12, 1927, at 2:15 p.m.

Catalogue Numbers 186 to 381 Inclusive

BLUE AND WHITE, AND DECORATED
CHINESE PORCELAINS

186. Two Blue and White Birdseed Cups   *Ch'ien-lung*
Semi-ovoid, delicately painted in underglaze cobalt with peonies in a thick bed of leaves; double ring handles reserved in white. One with cover.

187. Blue and White "Soft Paste" Birdseed Cup
Yung Chêng
Finely painted in underglaze cobalt with peasants and fishermen in a rocky landscape. Has stand.

Diameter, 3 inches

188. Three Snuff Bottles
One in glass with painted landscape decoration, one in cloisonné enamel, and a third in cloisonné of the *Ch'ien-lung* period.

189. Five Small Three-color Dishes   *K'ang-hsi*
Three six-sided and two pentagonal. Ornamented with sprays of hawthorn and kylins reserved in aubergine and white in a camellia-leaf ground with yellow borders.

190. Six Small Green Hawthorn Trapezoidal Dishes
K'ang-hsi
Reserved in white with *mei* blossoms in grounds of camellia-leaf green, bordered in yellow.

191. FAMILLE-ROSE ROUGE BOX, AND TWO VASES

[A] Enameled in rose-pink, the lid reserved with figures of a musician and four children. [B] Ovoid covered jar enameled in rose Pompadour, and with two landscape reserves. [C] Ovoid vase with engraved rose-pink enamel decoration and painted with a spray of flowers.

Diameter of [a], 3¾ inches
Height of [b], 4½ inches
Height of [c], 5 inches

192. OVOID VASE   *Chia Ch'ing*

Decorated with scrollings of lotus and peonies reserved in green in a black ground. Teakwood cover.

Height, 6 inches

193. FAMILLE-ROSE TEA-CUP AND SAUCER   *Ch'ien-lung*

Decorated in colors and gilding with reserves of pink peonies in diaper grounds, and centred with the figure of a kylin amid blossoms.

194. TWO ROSE-RED PLATES   *Tao Kuang*

Each with a central reserve depicting flowers and hens, the borders with smaller reserves painted with landscapes, birds and flowers.

Diameters, 9 inches and 11 inches

195. COVERED BOX WITH DRAGON DECORATION   *Yung Chêng*

Ground in pale cobalt-blue reserved in liver color with an imperial dragon writhing after the jewel amid clouds. Six-character seal mark of Yung Chêng at base.

Diameter, 5 inches

196. BLUE AND WHITE COVERED ROUGE BOX

Circular cushion-shape; the sides and lid decorated with imperial dragons pursuing the jewel amid clouds. Apocryphal six-character mark of Chêng Hua.

Diameter, 4¾ inches

72

197. DECORATED EGGSHELL PORCELAIN TEA-CUPS AND SAUCERS
Mostly of the *Tao Kuang* period. Comprising a pair of small
cups and saucers with diaper ornament and floral reserves;
pair of larger cups and saucers with hens and peony blossoms in the *famille-rose;* covered cup and saucer with *famille-rose* floral decoration and apocryphal mark of *Yung
Chêng; famille-rose* cup and saucer with floral ornament;
rose-pink cup and saucer [cup repaired]; a cup, and two
saucers.

198. BLUE AND WHITE "RICE GRAIN" COVERED SPICE BOX
Ch'ien-lung
Box and cover decorated in underglaze cobalt with borders of
ju-i heads and formalized plantain leaves, between which
appear bands of the translucent "rice grain" pattern perforated in the paste. Has stand.   *Diameter, 4½ inches*

199. BLUE AND WHITE GINGER JAR   *Ch'ien-lung*
Beneath an ivory-white glaze with streaky colorless crackle
is painted an arboretum with rockery, bamboos, chrysanthemums and other flowering shrubs, in a rich cobalt-blue.
Has teakwood cover and stand.   .   *Height, 7½ inches*

200. BLUE AND WHITE "SOFT PASTE" VASE   *Ch'ien-lung*
Slender ovo-cylindrical body with short neck. Beneath a
brilliant milk-white glaze with fugitive brown crackle are
painted in underglaze cobalt, a peony bush and flying insects.
Height, 8½ inches

201. TWO TALL-NECKED BOTTLES WITH ANIMAL DECORATION
K'ang-hsi
Globular body with tall chimney neck; decorated in liver
color beneath a brilliant white glaze, each with three figures
of squatting animals.
Height, 8½ inches; and 9½ inches

73

202. CYLINDRICAL VASE WITH FLORAL ORNAMENT

Yung Chêng

With tall incurved neck. Soft flour-white glaze decorated in the *famille-rose* enamels with a branch of peonies, hawthorn and asters.

Height, 9¾ inches

203. THREE-COLOR PLATE *K'ang-hsi*

Ground of camellia-leaf green, decorated with whorls and supporting hawthorn blossoms, emblems of the *Pa Pao* and running stags in yellow and aubergine. Splash of green glazing on base [slightly repaired].

Diameter, 10 inches

204. ROSE-PINK BOWL *Ch'ien-lung*

Exterior enameled in rose and painted with three kylins playing with the sacred jewel, between bands of formal ornament. Six-character seal mark of the reign in underglaze blue.

Diameter, 7¾ inches

205. BLUE AND WHITE JAR *Chia Ching*

Ovoid body with embryonic neck. Richly painted in Mohammedan-blue with jewel-like pendants of flowers, utensils, etc.; the base depicting five horses in flight over the waves. Six-character mark of *Chia Ching*. [Neck repaired.]

Height, 8½ inches

206. BLUE AND WHITE COVERED VASE *Wan Li*

With well-defined foot. Decorated in underglaze Mohammedan-blue with two imperial dragons in pursuit of the jewel, with bands of peony blossoms amid leaf scrollings and borders of *lei wên*. Six-character mark of *Wan Li*.

Length, 9½ inches

207. BLUE AND WHITE JAR   *Wan Li*

Ovoid body with embryonic neck. Richly painted in Mohammedan-blue with jewel like pendants of flowers, utensils, etc.,
the base depicting five horses in flight over the waves. Six-
character mark of *Wan Li.*

Height, 9½ *inches*

208. BLUE AND WHITE OVOID COVERED VASE   *K'ang-hsi*

Tall ovoid body decorated in rich underglaze cobalt with *ju-i*
head lappets, reserved with blossoms pendent from neck and
base. Has stand. [Cover repaired.]

Height, 10 *inches*

209. BLUE AND WHITE OVOID COVERED VASE   *K'ang-hsi*

Tall ovoid body decorated in rich underglaze cobalt with *ju-i*
head lappets, reserved with blossoms pendent from neck and
base. Has stand. [Cover repaired.]

Height, 10 *inches*

210. THREE FAMILLE-ROSE PLATES   *Tao Kuang*

One with floral decoration and ruby back; and two others
decorated with blossoms and birds in brilliant *famille-rose*
enamels.   *Diameters,* 7 *inches,* 8 *inches,* 9 *inches*

211. GALLIPOT WITH FLORAL DECORATION   *Tao Kuang*

Brilliant white glaze enameled with two butterflies and a
spray of pink and yellow blossoms, in the manner of *Yung
Chêng.*   *Height,* 8¼ *inches*

212. BLUE AND WHITE GINGER JAR   *Ch'ien-lung*

Beautifully painted in underglaze cobalt with bunches of
peaches and pomegranates, with borders of *ju-i* form lappets
at the neck and wave pattern about the foot. Beautiful warm
ivory glaze with pale irregular crackle. Carved teakwood
cover.   *Height,* 7 *inches*

75

213. FAMILLE-ROSE EGGSHELL PLATE   *Ch'ien-lung*

Displaying the seated figure of a maiden instructing two children; pea-green rose and blue diaper borders with three reserves of peony branches. [Repaired.]

Diameter, 8¼ inches

214. FAMILLE-ROSE SEMI-EGGSHELL PORCELAIN PLATE

Chia Ch'ing

Allover design of diaper scrollings overlaid with *mei* blossoms centred with a pink peony. [Slight repairs.]

Diameter, 8 inches

215. FAMILLE-ROSE PORCELAIN PLATE   *Chia Ch'ing*

Enameled with figures of two ladies in a garden and two children with a fishing rod; border of yellow and rose diapers each with four floral reserves.

Diameter, 9 inches

216. FAMILLE-ROSE PORCELAIN PLATE   *Chia Ch'ing*

Patterned in gold with lotus scrollings enclosing four leaf-shaped reserves with figures and *mei* blossoms in a central medallion. Rose diaper borders with floral reserves. [Repaired.]

Diameter, 8½ inches

217. BLUE AND WHITE HAWTHORN GINGER JAR   *K'ang-hsi*

Painted in deep cobalt-blue with a ground portraying the cracking ice, above which are spread ascending and descending sprays of *mei* blossoms, reserved in white. Finely chiseled metal cover and teakwood stand.

Height, 9 inches

76

218. BLUE AND WHITE BALUSTER VASE   *K'ang-hsi*

Decoration finely painted in underglaze cobalt, portraying a mandarin and attendants, with a waiting horse and servant, beside willows and pine trees. Six-character mark of *Chia Ch'ing* within double ring.

Height, 10 *inches*

219. BLUE AND WHITE OVOID DRAGON VASE   *K'ang-hsi*

Slender body with short neck. Under brilliant white glaze are painted in cobalt-blue two imperial five-color dragons. Six-character *nien hao* of *K'ang-hsi*. Has stand.

Height, 9 *inches*

220. BLUE AND WHITE BALUSTER VASE

Decorated in rich cobalt with a mountainous landscape. Apocryphal mark; *ch'ien* [a jewel] in underglaze-blue.

Height, 10 *inches*

221. FAMILLE-ROSE GARNITURE OF FIVE PIECES   *Tao Kuang*

Comprising three covered *potiches* and two beaker vases. Decoration in the *famille-rose* colors of intertwining stems of peonies, hawthorn, etc., amid which are figures of birds. [Covers slightly chipped.]

Height of potiches, 11 *inches*
Height of beaker, 9 *inches*

222. BLUE AND WHITE SEMI-EGGSHELL VASE   *Ch'ien-lung*

Akin to the so-called "soft paste" type. Granular milk-white glaze, beneath which is finely painted in underglaze cobalt, a wooded landscape scene with rockery, habitations and figures. [Kiln cracks at lip.]

Height, 15½ *inches*

77

223. BLUE AND WHITE "SOFT PASTE" VASE   *Ch'ien-lung*
Tall ovoid body with wide flaring mouth, coated with a fine
vellum-like white glaze of great brilliancy beneath which
appear chimeras writhing amid a mass of scrolling branches;
with bands of diaper and *ju-i* ornament and floral scrolls
and roundels about the neck.   *Height, 16 inches*

[Illustrated]

224. FAMILLE-ROSE LANTERN-SHAPED VASE   *Yung Chêng*
Quadrilateral, with pierced square top and base decorated
in rose and cobalt-blue; the sides enameled in *famille-rose*
colors with birds and butterflies, flying over peony and
hawthorn bushes. Semi-eggshell porcelain. [Slight crack
at base.]   *Height, 13½ inches*

78

225. BLUE AND WHITE BALUSTER MARINE VASE WITH
       PEACHBLOOM DECORATION   *K'ang-hsi*

Graceful body invested with a pure flour-white glaze, beneath which appear in peachbloom a huge four-clawed dragon and a carp struggling amid a swell of cobalt-blue waves dashing against a rock of celadon hue. Over the water are scattered flower-heads. Six-character mark of the reign within a double ring.

Height, 16½ inches

226. BLUE AND WHITE VASE WITH BULBOUS NECK
                                         Ch'ien-lung

Tall ovoid body, with flaring foot and cup-shaped mouth. Painted in underglaze blue with a wooded rocky landscape beside a lake, and invested with a creamy glaze with streaky *café-au-lait* crackle. [Repaired.]

Height, 18½ inches

227. BLUE AND WHITE TALL-NECKED VASE   *K'ang-hsi*

Ovoid body with tall beaker neck and flaring foot. Embellished in underglaze-cobalt with numerous compartments painted alternately with landscapes and groups of utensils, with formal floral borders at rim and foot. Mark: Double ring. Has stand.

Height, 18½ inches

228. FAMILLE-VERTE COVERED VASE, PARTLY OF THE K'ANG-HSI
       PERIOD

Tall baluster-shaped body of quatrefoil section with cover similarly. Decorated in the *famille-verte* colors with eight panels depicting rocky lakeside landscape, ducks amid water plants, sprays of chrysanthemums, wild animals, etc.; the neck with utensils. [The body as far as the shoulder appears to be of the *K'ang-hsi* period.]

Height, 26 inches

79

SINGLE-COLOR PORCELAINS, POTTERY

229. LUNG CH'ÜAN MINIATURE JAR   *Sung*

Spheroidal body with short neck. Dull celadon glaze with broad *café-au-lait* crackle. Has stand.

Height, 3 inches

230. WHITE PORCELAIN WRITER'S RECEPTACLE   *K'ang-hsi*

Hemispherical, with embryonic neck. Soft flour-white glaze beneath which are molded three roundels formed by the bodies of archaistic scrolled chimera figures. Rare. Six-character mark of the reign in underglaze blue. Has stand.

Diameter, 5 inches

[Illustrated]

231. WRITER'S RECEPTACLE   *K'ang-hsi*

Globular bowl invested with a buff glaze of soft lustre broken by a broad black crackle figure.

Diameter, 3¾ inches

232. LANG YAO WRITER'S DISH   *K'ang-hsi*

Circular, with finely modeled foot; foot and interior with greenish-white crackled glaze. Exterior invested with a rich coat of strawberry-pink glaze finely mottled and having a *peau d'orange* texture. [Slight kiln cracks.]

Diameter, 5 inches

[Illustrated]

233. LANG YAO BOWL   *K'ang-hsi*

Circular, with fluted sides and well formed ring foot. Glazed within and without with a thick and unctuous covering of ox-blood red darkening in the hollows of the flutes and thinning away to a watery plasma around the lip. [Slight nick at lip.]

Diameter, 7¼ inches

[Illustrated]

No. 230

No. 232

No. 233

No. 230. White Porcelain Writer's Receptacle
No. 232. Lang Yao Writer's Dish
No. 233. Lang Yao Bowl

234. LANG YAO OVOID VASE   *K'ang-hsi*

Light buff paste coated with a warm and viscous glaze of mottled strawberry-pink of the *lang yao* family, terminating in a thick coagulated ring about the foot. [Neck ground and repaired with metal.] Has stand.

Height, 6¾ inches

235. WRITER'S BOWL AND PEACHBLOOM AMPHORA

[A] Globular, with *lang yao* glaze fluctuating from cherry-red to liver color. [B] Strawberry-pink and heavily flecked with green spots. Have stands.

[a] Height, 3 inches
[b] Height, 6 inches

236. BOTTLE-FORM VASE   *Ming*

Depressed body with tall neck; orange-brown clay invested with a thick turquoise-blue glaze with purple and greenish markings and *peau d'orange* surface. Has stand.

Height, 4¾ inches

237. TWO IRIDESCENT POTTERY COVERED JARS   *Han*

One molded with a band of running animals about the shoulder; cover centred with a molded quatrefoil within scrolled borders. One with traces of cucumber-green, the other with a lime-yellow iridescence.

Height, 5½ inches

238. IRIDESCENT POTTERY INCENSE BURNER   *Han*

Cauldron-shaped, with three stump feet; two lug handles and cover. Cucumber-green glaze with earthy incrustations and iridescence. Cover molded with scrolled stems and bird figures. Has stand.

Height, 7 inches

239. SANG-DE-BOEUF WRITER'S RECEPTACLE   *K'ang-hsi*

Buff ware clothed with a thick and viscous ox-blood glaze —with finely pitted surface, the interior glazed white and exhibiting a *café-au-lait* sharkskin crackle.

Diameter, 3¾ inches

240. KUANGTUNG STONEWARE BOWL OF CHÜN YAO TYPE

Circular, with sharply retreating sides.   Chocolate-brown body invested with a sky-blue glaze, thickly pitted.

Diameter, 6½ inches

241. LANG YAO GALLIPOT

Brilliant mottled *sang-de-boeuf* glaze thinning at the neck to a transparency. Teakwood stand.

Height, 8½ inches

242. POTTERY COVERED JAR   *Ming*

Inverted pear-shape with wide mouth and hat cover; lid and neck molded with borders of *ju-i* form lappets; the sides rudely decorated with a landscape and rockery, in turquoise and ale-brown, on an aubergine ground. [Repaired.]

Height, 6½ inches

243. SANG-DE-BOEUF OVOID VASE   *K'ang-hsi*

Slender body with a short flaring neck [repaired with copper]. Rich oily glaze of ox-blood red, finely pitted and exhibiting a regular dark crackle, thinning away to a greenish watery plasma about the well-formed foot.

Height, 8 inches

244. CHÜN YAO TWO-HANDLED VASE   *Sung*

Pear-shaped, with scrolled loop handles at neck. Sky-blue glaze with purplish-blue blotches and broken by a regular *truité* crackle. Has stand.

Height, 6 inches

245. SANG-DE-BOEUF CRACKLE JAR

Pear-shaped, with wide neck; brilliant glaze thinning to a watery color at the lip, with broad crackle.

Height, 8 inches

246. STRAWBERRY-RED GALLIPOT   *Ch'ien-lung*

Thick, mottled, and beautifully flecked glaze of the *lang yao* family, terminating evenly about the foot and thinning away to a watery ring at the neck.   *Height, 7 inches*

247. ROBIN'S-EGG-BLUE VASE   *Tao Kuang*

Club-shaped, with flaring neck; decorated with wavy scroll-ings. Apocryphal four-character mark of *Ch'ien-lung*.

Height, 6½ inches

248. PAIR CORAL-RED BALUSTER VASES   *Tao Kuang*

Graceful body with flaring foot. *Soufflé* orange-red glaze.

Height, 8 inches

249. LANG YAO BOTTLE   *K'ang-hsi*

Inverted pear-shaped body, with tall neck. Fine paste of light buff, evenly clothed with a beautiful and softly polished glaze of cherry-red thinning at the mouth to leave a ring of white. Has stand.

Height, 9 inches

[Illustrated]

250. BOWL WITH SKY-BLUE GLAZE   *Yüan*

Circular, with sharply retreating sides; dark brown body coated with a thick and viscous sky-blue glaze with striated effects, and purple about the rim.

Diameter, 7¼ inches

[Illustrated]

No. 249

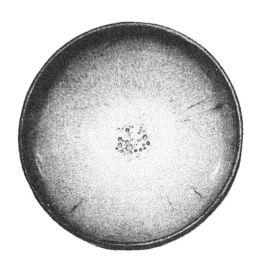

No. 250

No. 249. Lang Yao Bottle
No. 250. Bowl with Sky-blue Glaze

251. STRAWBERRY-PINK GALLIPOT   *Ch'ien-lung*

Delicate glaze, thinning over the shoulder and foot to a speckled effect and spread warmly about the waist. [Slight repairs to lip.]

Height, 7 inches

252. SKY-BLUE WRITER'S RECEPTACLE   *Ch'ien-lung*

Globular, invested with a pale ultramarine glaze ornamented with a *truité* black crackle. With cover and stand.

Diameter, 3¾ inches

253. WHITE PORCELAIN VASE WITH TRANSLUCENT DESIGN
Ch'ien-lung

Ovoid body with wide flaring neck; decorated like the "rice grain" bowls with a pattern of flowers and short scrolling branches, molded about the shoulder and foot and perforated in the paste about the neck and body. [Lip chipped.]

Height, 9½ inches

254. LANG YAO BEAKER VASE   *Ch'ien-lung*

Ovoid body with flaring foot and tall beaker neck. Unctuous pitted glaze of deep strawberry-red with velvety *peau d'orange* surface and finishing evenly at the foot. Has stand.

Height, 9½ inches

255. CHERRY-RED GALLIPOT   *Ch'ien-lung*

Warm even glaze of pure strawberry color with a dark flush on the neck and shoulder of one side, and terminating with beautiful regularity at neck and foot.

Height, 7½ inches

256. VASE WITH PIERCED FOOT   *Sung*

Baluster vase with corrugated loop handles, on five-sided ridged foot, pierced with five diamond-shaped apertures. Brownish-blue glaze with *flambé* effects. [Neck repaired.]

Height, 8 inches

257. LANG YAO BOTTLE   *K'ang-hsi*

Globular body with tall neck. Fine buff ware thickly coated with a beautiful strawberry glaze of the *lang yao* family terminating evenly about the foot. Has stand. [Lip repaired.]

Height, 8 inches

258. ANCIENT CHINESE COVERED JAR

Pear-shaped, of oval section; cover with melon finial. Decoration of archaic angular scrollings forming *t'ao-t'ieh* heads engraved on the body and chiseled in raised bands about the neck and lid. Has stand.

Height, 12 inches

259. NANKIN-YELLOW IMPERIAL DRAGON VASE   *Ch'ien-lung*

Globo-cylindrical, with tall flaring neck. Decorated under a golden-brown glaze with the incised figure of a five-clawed dragon and bats flying amid amorphous clouds. [Foot slightly nicked.]

Height, 12 inches

260. LANG YAO BOTTLE   *K'ang-hsi*

Globular ovoid body with tall cylindrical neck, invested with a buff polished glaze of blood-red, unctuous and warm to the touch. Has stand.

Height, 8 inches

261. NANKIN YELLOW BOTTLE-FORM VASE   *Ch'ien-lung*

Globular ovoid body with tall neck. Fluctuating golden-yellow glaze with fugitive iridescence about the body and shoulder.

Height, 12½ inches

262. LANG YAO TALL-NECKED BOTTLE   *K'ang-hsi*

Spheroidal body with tall cylindrical neck and well turned foot. Coated with a glaze fluctuating from a mottled strawberry-pink to blood-red, the underfoot invested with a watery celadon glaze. Has stand.

Height, 9½ inches

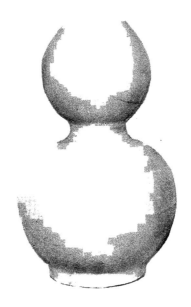

263. TING YAO DOUBLE-GOURD VASE   *Sung*

Delicately incised with blossoms emitting elaborate tendril scrollings, together with bands of fret meander motives and wave scrolls, beneath a rich ivory glaze with warm and polished patina.

Height, 12 *inches*

[Illustrated]

88

264. LANG YAO BALUSTER VASE   *K'ang-hsi*

Grayish buff body invested with a thick mottled glaze of deep strawberry-pink, with warm surface of *peau d'orange* texture and fluctuating tones. Has stand. [Neck repaired and rimmed in copper.]   *Height, 8¾ inches*

265. CHERRY-RED BOTTLE   *K'ang-hsi*

Globular, with tall cylindrical neck. Clothed with a brilliant glaze of deep red which leaves a white rim about the lip and terminates evenly about the foot. Has stand.

Height, 12½ inches

266. SANG-DE-BOEUF BOTTLE-FORM VASE   *K'ang-hsi*

Depressed globular body with tall wide neck. The glaze on the neck fluctuates from a thin strawberry-pink to a pigeon-blood red, assuming a grayish and thicker tone as it flows over the shoulder; on the body the flow terminates rudely along two ridges which appear in the paste; the whole is broken by a beautiful dark crackle at one of its sides. The vase is a ceramic curiosity.   *Height, 15 inches*

Duveen Brothers Loan Exhibition, January and February, 1907

267. OVERBAKED ROSE-RED BOTTLE-FORM VASE   *Ch'ien-lung*

Pear-shaped, with tall cylindrical neck; dull glaze of deep rose Pompadour hue, with areas of brown.

Height, 15 inches

268. SANG DE BOEUF PEAR-SHAPED VASE   *K'ang-hsi*

Tall jar with wide mouth and well formed foot. Viscous and oily glaze of fluid ox-blood red mottled towards the base and thinning away at the neck to leave a white ring; one side bears a regular crackle. [Repaired.]   *Height, 16½ inches*

89

269. LANG YAO BOTTLE-FORM VASE *K'ang-hsi*

Globular body with tall neck, rimmed with a white lip. Fine yellowish-white paste, covered with a beautiful and delicately fluctuating glaze changing from blood-red to a deep strawberry color and mottled where coagulation commences about the foot. Has stand.

Height, 17 inches

[Illustrated]

270. LANG YAO BALUSTER VASE *K'ang-hsi*

Beautifully proportioned body with finely turned neck. Buff body covered by a rich fluctuating glaze of strawberry-pink, mottled and bearing on the shoulder a single splash of peach-bloom. The glaze is velvety and finely pitted, with a soft patina to the hand.

Height, 17 inches

[Illustrated]

271. PAIR POTTERY EQUESTRIAN FIGURES *Ming*

Two officials in armor mounted on war horses; arched base. Glazed in cucumber-green, pale-brown and aubergine.

Heights, 13½ inches and 15 inches

272. PAIR KYLIN POTTERY FIGURINES

Male and female *Fu* dog with raised paw, on oblong plinth base. Glazed in aubergine, turquoise-blue and a yellowish-buff.

Height, 20 inches

273. CHINESE BRONZE PEAR-SHAPED VASE *Han* [?]

Of oval section, with high foot. Chiseled in relief with two *t'ao t'ieh*, or ogres.

Height, 7 inches

No. 269

No. 270

No. 269. Lang Yao Bottle-form Vase
No. 270. Lang Yao Baluster Vase

PASSEMENTERIE, DAMASKS, BROCATELLES
BROCADES AND VELVETS, INCLUDING SEVERAL
MAGNIFICENT NEEDLEPAINTED COPES

274. SIX PRIMROSE-YELLOW SILK TASSELS

Louis XVI Period

Peg tops of yellow and salmon-pink, yellow silk skirts.

275. SET OF FOUR SALMON-PINK AND YELLOW SILK TASSELS

Louis XV Period

Spiraled tops, shoulders in salmon-pink, and skirts of yellow.

276. SIX YELLOW SILK AND GOLD TASSELS *Louis XVI Period*

Knotted yellow and gold cords, fluffy skirts of yellow silk and gold thread.

277. SET OF EIGHT YELLOW SILK AND GOLD TASSELS

Louis XV Period

With double cords and fringed skirts of yellow silk and gold thread.

278. SET OF FIVE CRIMSON SILK TASSELS

French, Louis XIV Period

Spiraled red and yellow heads and knotted skirts of rose and shell-pink silk.

279. SILK AND SILVER TASSEL   *French, XVII Century*

Important tassel with latticed body of silver wire and shoulder knots and skirts of blue, yellow, and pink and white.

280. LOT OF TEN ASSORTED SILK TASSELS   *XVIII Century*

Comprising one in blue and white, three in rose-pink, three in yellow, one in green and white, one in salmon-pink, and one in rose and white.

281. EMERALD-GREEN VELVET PANEL WITH A PAPAL
ESCUTCHEON   *Genoese, XVII Century*

Rich close pile velvet, of dark tone; centred with an *appliqué* papal escutcheon.

282. PAIR SILVER- AND SILK-EMBROIDERED SKY-BLUE DAMASK
AMICES   *French, Late XVII Century*

Damassé with a leaf design and embroidered in silver thread with a floral motive enriched with sequins and surrounded by flower-heads in silk centred in silver. With silk cords and two beautiful silver tassels.

283. GOLD- AND SILK-EMBROIDERED ESCUTCHEON
Italian, Late XVIII Century

Within a wreath of laurel, an oval cartouche charged with *fleur-de-lys*, a mitre and an arm holding a pastoral staff, over which is a bend checky. Mounted on a silver-woven silk frontal.

284. PAIR GOLD- AND SILVER-EMBROIDERED ESCUTCHEONS
Spanish, XVII Century

Leaf-scrolled borders enclosing an oval cartouche exhibiting a church flanked by two vases of lilies in gold, in a latticed silver ground.

285. FOUR EPISCOPAL ESCUTCHEONS   *Italian Renaissance*

Each with leaf-scrolled golden shield, charged with a star surmounting a stag's head in an azure field, and with a black and gold bishop's hat having pendent *fiocci*.

286. RENAISSANCE GOLD AND SILVER SILK NEEDLEPAINTED
ORPHREY *Spanish, XV Century*
Developing four oblong panels enclosing round-arched
niches with cupolas and standing figures of SS. Peter, Barbara, Philip, and James.

Length, 5 feet 6 inches; width, 8½ inches

[Illustrated]

287. THREE GENOESE RUBY VELVET MANIPLES
Italian, XV Century
Beautiful specimens of the finest velvet with long silky pile.

*Vitall and Leopold Benguiat Collection, American Art Asso-
ciation, 1919*

288. GOLD NEEDLEPAINTED AND EMBROIDERED BOTTICELLI-
GREEN VELVET ORPHREY *Italian, XVI Century*
Beautiful velvet with symmetrical Renaissance leaf-scroll
embroidery in gold and silver threads, and four roundels
needlepainted in silver and gold overlaying colored silks,
with figures of St. Peter, St. Bartholomew, the Savior, and
St. Paul.

Length, 4 feet 4 inches; width, 7½ inches

[Illustrated]

289. TWO GOLD AND SILVER NEEDLEPAINTED ORPHREYS OF A
CHASUBLE *Italian, XV Century*
Finely worked in gold and silver thread and colored silks in
a *point d'Hongrie* stitch, with oblong panels enclosing Gothic
niches having figures of the Savior, St. Barbara, St. Andrew,
and two martyred saints, together with the escutcheon and
green hat of a bishop.

No. 286

No. 288

No. 286. Renaissance Gold and Silver Silk Needlepainted Orphrey

No. 288. Gold Needlepainted and Embroidered Botticelli-green
Velvet Orphrey

290. EMERALD-GREEN VELVET PANEL

Genoese, Early XVII Century

A small panel in beautiful preservation, of this rare deep toned velvet. *Length, 32 inches; width, 23 inches*

291. DRAP D'ARGENT CHINOISERIE BROCADE TABLE COVER

Louis XV Period

Gray ground, beautifully woven in pastel-colored silk and cloth-of-silver thread with mounds of rockery supporting flowering hawthorn shrubs and winding between stems of golden flowers. *39 inches square*

292. GENOESE JARDINIÈRE VELVET CHASUBLE

Italian, XVII Century

Bold design *à deux hauteurs* in wine-red, pale green, mauve and taupe of huge upstanding floral sprays supporting scrolling branches of flowers, beneath scrolled canopies of leafage.

[Illustrated]

293. RENAISSANCE MOSS-GREEN AND GOLDEN-YELLOW CUT VELVET PANEL *Italian, circa* 1600

Yellow ground richly patterned with a jardinière of blossoms and short scrolling branches of tulips, pomegranates and leafage *à deux hauteurs,* with rosetted leaf-scrolled borders.

Length, 30 inches; width, 21 inches

294. LEAF-GREEN FIGURED VELVET ARMORIAL CHASUBLE

Genoese, Late XVI Century

Sumptuous velvet with pale yellow tones and *frappé* with allover designs of looped lattices and quatrefoils, tiny S-scrolls and pellets; *appliqué* with a Spanish embroidered escutcheon of the sixteenth century charged with castles and a lion passant.

No. 292. Genoese Jardinière Velvet Chasuble

295. GOLD- AND SILVER-EMBROIDERED IVORY SILK ALTAR
     CLOTH   *French, XVII Century*

White silk, beautifully worked in gold and silver thread and
colored silks, with a border of scrolling branches of brilliant
blossoms, sprays of tulips and carnations at the corners and
a central sunburst with I H S entangled in a circular garland
of carnations and iris.

Depth, 44 inches; length, 72 inches

296. CYPRESS-GREEN VELVET TABLE RUNNER
                                       Genoese, XVI Century

Composed of pieced fragments of this rare tone of silken
velvet, with deep metallic lustre. Trimmed with gold galloon.

Length, 57 inches; width, 22 inches

297. PAIR SUMPTUOUS WINE-RED VELVET AND GOLD
     BROCATELLE DALMATICS *Spanish, Late XVI Century*

Silky velvet with long pile and softly glittering ruby tones;
with bands and apparels of rare leaf-green brocatelle developing in gold colors a pattern of interlacing leaf arabesques. With green silk tassels.

298. SIX ROSE-CRIMSON CUT VELVET COVERS
                                 Genoese, Louis XIV Period

Rose-red satin ground, woven *à deux hauteurs* with a beautiful spreading device of flowers and leafage beneath an arch
of ribbon branches and foliage, and pairs of nodding roses.
Trimmed with gold galloon. The backs of seventeenth century crimson brocatelle.

Length, 31 inches; width, 28 inches

*Vitall and Leopold Benguiat Collection, American Art Asso-
ciation, 1919*

299. GOLD BOUCLÉ BROCATELLE AND EMBROIDERED VELVET
     CHASUBLE   *Venetian Renaissance*

Rare field of ivory and golden-yellow brocatelle of the early sixteenth century patterned with leafage and floral scrollings, the latter *bouclé* with looped gold threads; border and orphreys of Genoese ruby velvet *appliqués* with a symmetrical Renaissance design of vases of honeysuckle and pairs of clasped S- and C-scrollings in ivory and golden-yellow silk outlined with gold thread.

Vitall and Leopold Benguiat Collection, American Art Association, 1919

300. ROYAL JARDINIÈRE VELVET VALANCE
                                Genoese, Louis XIV Period

Three pieces. Design on an écru satin ground of symmetrical baskets of blossoms and leafage alternating with scrolled and strapped framework and woven *à deux hauteurs* in claret, tawny-orange, yellow, fawn and olive-green. Trimmed with green silk fringe.

Total length, 20 *feet* 6 *inches; depth,* 2 *feet*

301. SILVER EMBROIDERY AND VENETIAN LEAF-GREEN SILK
     BROCADE CHASUBLE

Of satin, brocaded in pastel colors and ivory with large floral sprays and broad latticed ribbon ornament; trimmed with silver lace galloon and centred with seventeenth century orphreys of sky-blue silk damask richly embroidered in silver and colored silks with rococo devices, bunches of leafage, delicate stems of flowers and a coroneted escutcheon, enriched with *paillettes.*

99

302. Appliqué Embroidered Rose-crimson Damask
Lambrequin   *Louis XIV Period*

Floral damask embellished with an *appliqué* design in yellow satin of interlacing strap scrollings and leafage forming a pendant of Louis XIV design. Trimmed with silk fringe.

Length, 6 feet 4 inches; width, 4 feet 3 inches

303. Gold- and Silver-embroidered Genoese Velvet Border
Italian, XVI Century

Developing in heavy gold and silver threads a Renaissance design of symmetrical strap scrollings interlacing with branches bearing pairs of pendent leaves.

Length, 4 feet 2 inches; width, 10 inches

304. Ruby-crimson Velvet Dorsal   *Genoese, XVI Century*

Three panels of superb Renaissance velvet with soft pile and crimson sheen. Mounted with gold galloon and fringe.

Length, 6 feet 10 inches; depth, 2 feet 3 inches

305. Jardinière Velvet Table Runner
Genoese, XVII Century

Bold recurring Louis XIV design of *corbeilles* of flowers and leafage in claret, tawny orange, olive-yellow and green, in an écru satin ground. *Length, 8 feet 5 inches; width, 19 inches*

306. Golden-yellow Satin Damask Cover
Italian, XVII Century

Four widths. Baroque design of rows of fantastic scrolled and latticed cornucopia-like forms, hung with leafage and interspersed with scattered wild flowers.

Length, 6 feet 7 inches; width, 7 feet 2 inches

307. Length of Genoese Ruby Velvet
Italian, XVII Century

Heavy silk velvet with close pile and deep wine-red tones.

Length, 12 feet 8 inches; width, 1 foot 9 inches

308. Four Crimson Velvet and Appliqué Drap d'Or Embroidery Column Hangings

Portuguese, XVII Century

Rich lustrous velvet with deep wine-red tones; enriched with a bold Louis XIV design in yellow and cloth-of-gold, exhibiting huge symmetrical floral sprays enclosed by ogivals of pointed leaves supporting pairs of pendent pomegranates.

Length, 11 yards 2 feet; width, 1 foot 8 inches

Vitall and Leopold Benguiat Collection, American Art Association, 1919

[Illustrated]

309. Crimson Velvet and Appliqué Drap d'Or Embroidered Valance

Pórtuguese, Early XVII Century

Comprising nine strips, forming sixteen points in all. Beautiful Genoese velvet of thick pile and rose sheen, *appliqué* in cloth-of-gold with symmetrical skeletonized sprays of leafage, fuchsias, and other blossoms, supported on an angular scroll with strapwork motive.

Total length, 11 yards 6 inches; depth, 2 feet 5 inches

Vitall and Leopold Benguiat Collection, American Art Association, 1919

No. 308

310. IMPERIAL GOLD- AND SILK-EMBROIDERED HANGING

Ch'ien-lung

Beautifully worked in gold thread and red and white silk with three huge writhing figures of imperial dragons pursuing the Sacred Jewel amid blue clouds, with waves and rockery at the base. Among the clouds appear flying birds and four Buddhist emblems. Navy-blue silk ground.

6 feet square

311. APPLIQUÉ EMBROIDERED RUBY VELVET VALANCE

Genoese, XVII Century

Four strips, comprising eighteen points. Shaped valance of dark thick-piled ruby velvet, trimmed with crimson fringe and enriched with a galloon *appliqué* of interlacing angular strapwork. *Length, 8 yards 2 feet; width, 1 foot 6 inches*

Vitall and Leopold Benguiat Collection, American Art Association, 1919

312. PAIR SILVER EMBROIDERY AND IVORY BROCADE DALMATICS

French, XVIII Century

Of beautiful Louise Quinze silk brocade, patterned with serpentine ribbons of golden foliage interlacing with trails of tiny green leaves with pendent blossoms in blue, claret and orange; banded, and with apparels of sky-blue silk damask, sumptuously embroidered with silver threads and colored silks, with detached scrolling floral stems and a coroneted escutcheon within bold leaf scrollings.

[Illustrated]

313. EMBROIDERED RUBY VELVET VALANCE

Genoese, XVI Century

Velvet with patina and wear of age, enriched in *appliqué* embroidery of gold galloon with a running cusped ornament embellished with *fleurs-de-lys*. Trimmed with gold fringe.

Total length, 20 feet 6 inches; depth, 1 foot 9 inches

No. 312. Pair Silver Embroidery and Ivory Brocade Dalmatics

314. SILVER-EMBROIDERED MOSS-GREEN VELVET AND SILK
DAMASK COPE *XVII Century*

Of jade-green damask with pattern of triple ribbon ogivals interlinked by coronets and enclosing symmetrical floral sprays; the hood and orphreys of velvet embroidered in silver with scalloped pendants and an aureole with the head of a saint.
Length, 9 feet 7 inches; depth, 4 feet 3 inches

315. RUBY VELVET HANGING *Genoese, XVI Century*

Beautiful portière of Renaissance velvet with fluctuating tones and patina of age. Banded with gold galloon.
Length, 6 feet 9 inches; width, 3 feet 5 inches

316. DRAP D'OR AND APPLIQUÉ VELVET EMBROIDERED BORDER
Portuguese, circa 1600

Yellow ground woven with gold threads and developing in *appliqué* crimson velvet a running pattern of interlacing voluted scrollings of leafage in the late Renaissance manner.
Total length, 11 *yards* 1 *foot; width,* 11 *inches*
Vitall. and Leopold Benguiat Collection, American Art Association, 1919

317. TWO EMBROIDERED RUBY VELVET VALANCES
Florentine, circa 1600

Developing on grounds of rich variously toned velvet, *appliqué* designs in metal threads and colored silks of running leaf scroll patterns of Renaissance type, enriched with tendrils. Trimmed with gold fringe.
Length of one, 9 *feet* 5 *inches; depth,* 18 *inches*
Length of one, 7 *feet* 3 *inches; depth,* 2 *feet* 2 *inches*

318. LENGTH OF RENAISSANCE RUBY VELVET
Genoese, XVI Century

Rich deep velvet showing a patina of wear, with linen border.
Length, 14 *feet* 8 *inches; width,* 1 *foot* 9 *inches*

319. RARE EMERALD-GREEN SILVER-WOVEN SILK TABLE COVER
Venetian, XVII Century

Graceful Louis Treize design of parallel undulating branches supporting rows of blossoms nodding in alternate directions; on a ground of basket pattern, brocaded in silver thread interlacing with floating wefts of green silk.

Length, 5 feet 4 inches; width, 3 feet 4 inches

320. CRIMSON VELVET HANGING   *Genoese, XVII Century*

Lustrous rose-crimson velvet with shimmering pile; three widths, in fine preservation.

Length, 7 feet; width, 5 feet 4 inches

321. PAIR LEAF-GREEN SILK DAMASK AND BROCATELLE
DALMATICS   *Italian, XVI Century*

Damask with small allover design of tiny short scrolling stems of leaves interspersed with scattered billets; with braid and apparels of early Renaissance brocatelle developing in an old-gold ground a pattern of ogivals enclosing symmetrical floral sprays in leaf-green and ivory.

Vitall and Leopold Benguiat Collection, American Art Association, 1919

322. LEAF-GREEN SILK DAMASK AND BROCATELLE CHASUBLE

To match the preceding.   *Italian, XVI Century*

323. BROCATELLE AND GENOESE RUBY VELVET ALTAR FRONTAL
Italian, XVI-XVII Century

A panel of sixteenth century rose and golden-yellow brocatelle with ogival design, enclosing pomegranates, which surmounts a frontal of brilliant seventeenth century velvet, trimmed with gold fringe and bands of contemporary *appliqué* gold embroidery. The frontal is finished off at the foot with a band of seventeenth century rose and yellow brocatelle.

Length, 7 feet 11 inches; width, 3 feet 5 inches

324. PAIR SILK-EMBROIDERED GENOESE RUBY VELVET COLUMN
HANGINGS   *Italian, circa* 1600

Rich velvet embroidered in floss silks outlined with *cordonnets* and deep braids in a symmetrical design of huge bunches
of foliage supporting brilliant blossoms and floral pendants
with *adossés* figures of exotic parrots.

Length, 9 feet 5 inches; width, 1 foot 7 inches

325. PAIR SILK-EMBROIDERED GENOESE. RUBY VELVET COLUMN
HANGINGS   *Italian, circa* 1600

Similar in design to the preceding, with variations of color.

Length, 9 feet 5 inches; width, 1 foot 7 inches

326. BOTTICELLI-GREEN VELVET VALANCE
Genoese, XVI Century

A rare and beautifully patinated strip of Renaissance velvet, with pale grass-green high-lights and surface of incredible softness. Trimmed with gold galloon and fringe.

Length, 12 feet 6 inches; width, 26 inches

327. RARE GOTHIC CRIMSON FERRONNERIE VELVET ALTAR
FRONTAL   *Venetian, Late XV Century*

Ground with rich and deep silky pile, *frappé* with a small allover design of short fern stems, and cut with bold ogival
octofoils supporting and enclosing vase-shaped pomegranate
devices. Trimmed with gold galloon and silk and gold
fringe.

Length, 6 feet 9 inches; width, 3 feet 4 inches

[Illustrated]

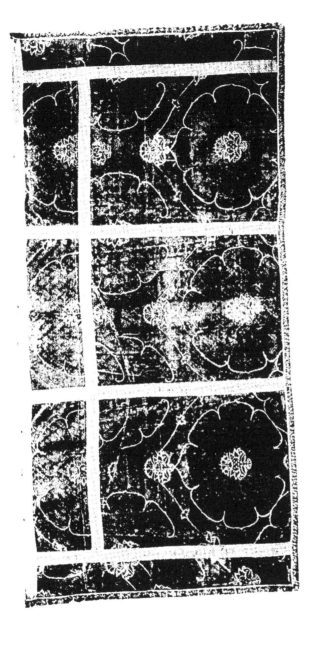

No. 327. Rare Gothic Crimson Ferronnerie Velvet Altar Frontal

328. VERY IMPORTANT VENETIAN GOTHIC CUT VELVET COPE
—— WITH ORPHREYS OF OPUS ANGLICANUM *XV Century*

The cope, in five widths of magnificent Venetian *ferronnerie* crimson velvet, with soft and silky pile, beautifully cut with delicate cinquefoil ogivals centred with small floral motives and supporting tiny blossoms festooned on threads. The orphreys, of fifteenth century English needlework are divided into ten oblong panels worked in gold and silver threads and colored silks; as follows: in the centre God the Father, and the Dove of the Holy Ghost; at sides St. Philip, St. Thomas, St. Mary Magdalen, St. Catherine tramping on the figure of Diocletian, St. Roch and the Angel of the Annunciation; the ends with small panels portraying angels with the pillar and instruments of the Flagellation.

Length, 8 feet 9 inches; depth, 3 feet 11 inches

Vitall and Leopold Benguiat Collection, American Art Association, 1919

[Illustrated]

NOTE: The needlework of this magnificent cope is representative of the period when the fame of English ecclesiastical embroidery, the *opus anglicanum*, was spread throughout Christendom. As far back as the thirteenth century, the cathedrals of France, Italy and Spain competed for the masterpieces of English handicraft; the great tradition dates back to Anglo-Saxon times, as was demonstrated by the discovery of the famous stole and maniple of St. Cuthbert in Durham cathedral, executed in 916 A. D. The rarity of existing examples in private hands need not be emphasized.

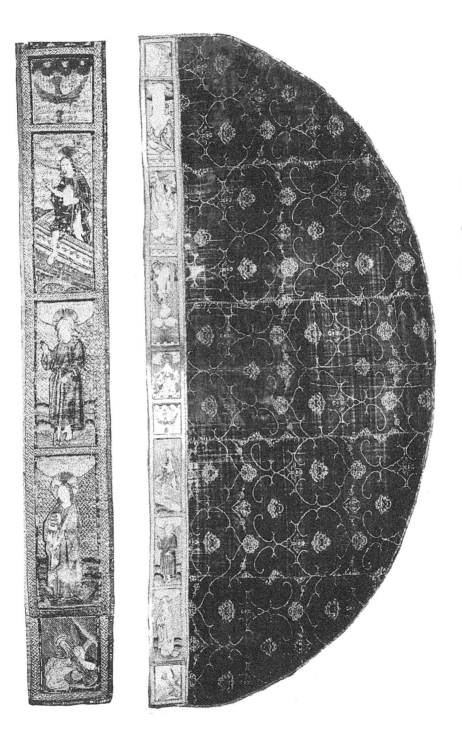

No. 328. Very Important Venetian Gothic Cut Velvet Cope with Orphreys of *Opus Anglicanum*

329. CRIMSON SATIN AND GOLD NEEDLEPAINTED COPE

Italian, XVI Century

Rich wine-crimson satin with orphreys needlepainted in gold
and silk, and divided into six panels with Renaissance and
Gothic niches enclosing figures of saints: St. Catherine of
Siena, St. Mary Magdalen, St. Martha of Bethany, St. Peter,
St. John and St. Andrew.

Length, 9 feet 10 inches; depth, 4 feet 7 inches

330. GENOESE RUBY VELVET AND GOLD-NEEDLEPAINTED COPE

Italian, XVI Century

The orphreys are superbly needlepainted with lateral gold
threads laid over colored silks and display eight oblong panels
with a symmetrical Renaissance ornament of clasped leaf
scrollings enclosing roundels with figures of the Virgin and
Child, St. Barbara, SS. Peter and Paul, Mark, Luke and
John, the hood with a beautiful portrayal of the enthroned
Madonna and Child. Sumptuous heavy velvet with dark
wine-red tones.

Length, 9 feet 2 inches; depth, 4 feet 4 inches

Vitall and Leopold Benguiat Collection, American Art Association, 1919

[Illustrated]

No. 330. Genoese Ruby Velvet and Gold-needlepainted Cope

331. GOLD NEEDLEPAINTED CISELÉ CRIMSON AND YELLOW
     VELVET ALTAR FRONTAL

Italian, Gothic-Renaissance Period

Composed of a frieze of thirteen panels needlepainted in
gold and silver thread and colored silks with the figures of
Christ and the Virgin Mary and male and female saints
with their attributes; the field of five breadths of velvet with
a golden-yellow ground and *ciselé* crimson pile developing
ogivals enclosing pineapple motives and supported on broad
curved bands emitting further branches of pineapple mo-
itves, scrolled leafage and cinquefoil blossoms. Trimmed
with gold galloon and fringe.

Length, 8 feet 6 inches; depth, 3 feet 6 inches

*Vitall and Leopold Benguiat Collection, American Art Asso-
ciation, 1919*

[Illustrated]

332. SET OF ROSE-CRIMSON AND YELLOW SILK BROCATELLE
     PANELS   *Lucca, XVII Century*

Majestic design of huge symmetrical frameworks of scrolling branches interlaced with foliage and blossoms, looped
with circlets and enclosing large sprays of flowers. Fifteen
pieces.

Total length, 15 yards; width, 2 feet 6 inches

333. SET OF ROSE-CRIMSON AND YELLOW SILK BROCATELLE
     HANGINGS   *Lucca, XVII Century*

To match the preceding. Twenty pieces.

Total length, about 66½ yards; various widths

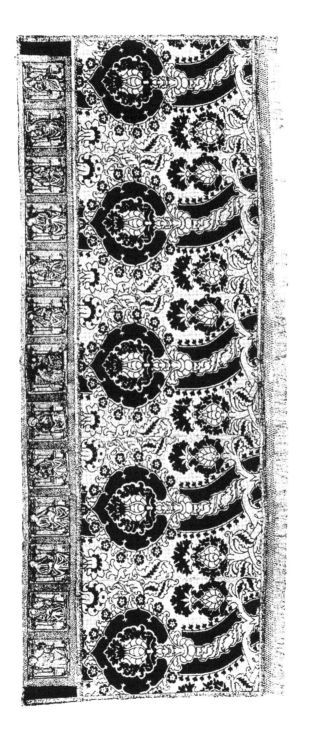

No. 331. Gold Needlepainted Ciselé Crimson and Yellow Altar Frontal

334. GENOESE RUBY VELVET AND NEEDLEPAINTED COPE

Italian, XVI Century

Of superb deep ruby velvet of the late sixteenth or early seventeenth century, in beautiful preservation, trimmed with golden-yellow brocatelle; orphreys needlepainted in gold and silver thread and colored silks with seven panels enclosing figures of God the Father, St. Anne with the Virgin and Child, St. Peter, St. Lawrence, St. Paul and two saintly bishops, together with original morse displaying coat of arms between symbolic chalices.

Length, 9 feet 11 inches; depth, 4 feet 3 inches

Vitall and Leopold Benguiat Collection, American Art Association, 1919

[Illustrated]

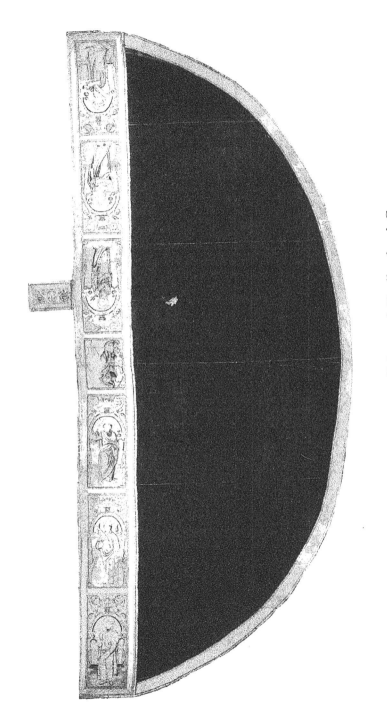

No. 334. Genoese Ruby Velvet and Needlepainted Cope

335. IVORY GOLD- AND SILK BROCADED COPE

French, XVIII Century

Damassé with a trellis design and woven with serpentine trails of salmon-pink, claret, yellow and other pastel-colored flowers and rococo fan motives in gold thread entwined in spirals of blue ribbon. With hood.

Length, 10 feet; depth, 4 feet 10 inches

336. ROYAL DRAP D'ARGENT JARDINIÈRE VELVET TABLE COVER

XVII Century

Beautiful fabric with ribbed ground of silver and tan threads; delicate raised design in pastel shades of lavender, rose-red and aquamarine, involving large symmetrical spade-shaped floral trophies encircled by scrolled and latticed branches with pendent leafage and blossoms.

Length, 6 feet 5 inches; width, 5 feet 3 inches

[Illustrated]

337. NINE LENGTHS OF ROSE-CRIMSON AND YELLOW SILK BROCATELLE *Lucca, Louis XIV Period*

Interesting design of serpentine trails of husks enriched with foliage and supporting pendent leaf sprays, alternate ones centring a sun in splendor, the emblem of King Louis XIV.

Total length, 22 yards 1 foot; width, 1 foot

338. TWO CRIMSON SILK DAMASK HANGINGS

Louis XIII Period

Elegant symmetrical design of frames of leafage linked by coronets, and enclosing sprays of blossoms alternating with vases of roses and carnations; the former flanked by *adossés* song birds, the latter by figures of peacocks.

Length of one, 9 feet; width, 8 feet 5 inches
Length of one, 9 feet; width, 8 feet 4 inches

No. 336. Royal Drap d'Argent Jardinière Velvet Table Cover

339. GENOESE CRIMSON VELVET HANGING

Italian, XVI Century

Seven widths of beautiful Renaissance velvet with fluctuating rose tones; bordered and cross-banded with two rows of gold galloon.

Height, 9 feet 3 inches; width, 11 feet 4 inches

340. WHITE AND GOLD BROCADE COPE   *Louis XVI Period*

Ground of white silk woven with stripes and floating weft threads in gold and silver, and brocaded with tiny sprays, circular garlands and spiraled trails of mauve and red roses. Trimmed with gold galloon and fringe; has hood.

Length, 9 feet 7 inches; depth, 4 feet 8 inches

341. GENOESE CRIMSON VELVET AND BROCATELLE DALMATIC

Italian, XVI Century

Lustrous rose-crimson velvet patinated by age; with bands and apparels of old-gold brocatelle developing in rose a bold Gothic design of large ogivals enriched with latticed leafage and enclosing a pomegranate resting on scrolling foliage.

342. GENOESE CRIMSON VELVET AND BROCATELLE DALMATIC

Italian, XVI Century

Similar to the preceding.

343. PAIR GOLD-EMBROIDERED GENOESE RUBY VELVET
ANTEPENDIA   *Italian, circa* 1600

Beautiful deep-toned velvet bordered with a rich *appliqué* design in yellow and gold threads embellished with scrollings, flowers and leafage, centred with a coroneted lambrequin lined in silver and bearing sacred monogram A M; bordered on three sides with galloon.

Length, 12 feet; width, 4 feet 5 inches

344. TWO CRIMSON SILK DAMASK HANGINGS
                    Spanish or Italian, Late XVII Century
Gigantic design of opposed scrolling branches supporting
pairs of pomegranates and curling pointed leaves and sustaining at intervals huge symmetrical bouquets of flowers and
foliage.

Total length, about 13 yards 2 feet; width, 3 feet 3 inches

345. BEAUTIFUL GENOESE RUBY VELVET TABLE COVER
                              Italian, XVI Century
Three widths of magnificent velvet with soft heavy pile and
fluctuating rose tones. Bordered with gold galloon.

Length, 9 feet 3 inches; width, 5 feet 4 inches

346. SET OF ROSE-CRIMSON SILK BROCATELLE HANGINGS
                              Italian, XVII Century
Symmetrical design of imbricated ribbon strap-work, looped
with coronets, supporting large bunches of foliage and interlaced with scrolling branches of pendent blossoms. Bordered and banded with gold galloon. Sixteen pieces.

Total length, about 57 yards; width, 2 feet 6 inches

347. PAIR LARGE RENAISSANCE CRIMSON VELVET HANGINGS
                              Genoese, Early XVII Century
Heavy velvet with thick close pile; cross-banded and edged
with gold galloon and trimmed with fringe.

Length, 10 feet 7 inches; width, 5 feet 10 inches

*Vitall and Leopold Benguiat Collection, American Art Asso-
ciation, 1919*

119

348. EMERALD-GREEN VELVET ALTAR FRONTAL
Genoese, Late XVI or Early XVII Century

Magnificent velvet of rare brilliance and beautiful preservation. Mounted with cross-bandings of gold galloon and edging of gold galloon and fringe.

Length, 8 feet 10 inches; depth, 3 feet 8 inches

349. SET OF ~~FOUR~~ ROYAL LOUIS QUATORZE JARDINIÈRE VELVET HANGINGS *Genoese, XVII Century*

Developing on an ivory silk ground a symmetrical design *à deux hauteurs* of baskets of flowers and leafage enclosed between massed nosegays supported on frameworks of scrolled strap motives. In claret, tawny orange, fawn, and olive-green.

Length, 8 feet 3 inches; width, 3 feet 6 inches

[Illustrated]

350. ARMORIAL FIGURED LEAF-GREEN VELVET AND SILK DAMASK COPE *Italian, XVI Century*

Hood and orphreys of shimmering velvet with rich patina of yellowish tone, and *frappé* with an allover design of interlacing ribbons enclosing small floral devices; on this are *appliqué* three embroidered coroneted Spanish escutcheons. The cope is of rare damask developing a square rosetted lattice design enclosing single heart-shaped leaf motives.

Length, 9 feet 5 inches; depth, 4 feet 7 inches

351. PAIR ARMORIAL FIGURED LEAF-GREEN VELVET AND SILK DAMASK DALMATICS *Italian, XVI Century*

To match the preceding.

352. ARMORIAL FIGURED LEAF-GREEN VELVET AND SILK DAMASK CHASUBLE *Italian, XVI Century*

To match the preceding.

No. 349. Set of Four Royal Louis Quatorze Jardinière Velvet Hangings

353. PAIR ROSE-CRIMSON VELVET COLUMN HANGINGS
Genoese, Late XVI or Early XVII Century
Superb velvet with heavy rose tone, in good preservation.
Edged with gold galloon. *Length, 8 feet; width, 24 inches*

354. GOLDEN-YELLOW SATIN BROCATELLE-DAMASK HANGING
Italian, XVII Century
Woven in tan and golden-yellow and developing a large
spade-shaped mass of flowers and leafage enclosed within
double ogivals of leaves supporting masses of foliage and
pairs of pendent orchids. Four widths.
Length, 10 feet; width, 8 feet 4 inches

355. APPLIQUÉ EMBROIDERED AMBER VELVET VALANCE
Spanish, XVI Century
Patterned in velvet outlined in gold thread with a beautiful running design of broadly scrolling leafage bearing pendent fuchsias and fruits and enriched with tendrils; at centre and ends three coroneted escutcheons picked out in gold
thread. Trimmed with silver fringe.
Length, 10 feet; depth, 11 inches

356. APPLIQUÉ GOLD-EMBROIDERED RUBY VELVET HANGING
Portuguese, Early XVII Century
Beautifully worked with an *appliqué* of gold thread outlined
by cordonnets in a pattern of symmetrical skeletonized sprays
of leaves supporting sunflowers.
Length, 9 feet 3 inches; width, 21 inches

357. IMPORTANT RENAISSANCE CRIMSON VELVET PALACE
HANGING *Genoese, Late XVI Century*
Composed of five superb widths of *cinquecento* velvet with
close thick pile and lustrous rose tones, in remarkable preser-
vation. Bordered and banded with broad gold galloon.
Length, 13 feet 6 inches; width, 9 feet

122

358. IMPORTANT RENAISSANCE CRIMSON VELVET PALACE
         HANGING   *Genoese, Late XVI Century*
     Similar to the preceding, but generally deeper in tone.

Length, 13 feet 6 inches; width, 9 feet

359. LEAF-GREEN SILK DAMASK COPE
                              Venetian, Early XVI Century
     Woven with an interesting conventionalized bird device with-
     in an imbricated ogival ribbon motive covering the field; the
     hood and orphrey with an allover billet and sprig pattern.

Length, 10 feet; depth, 4 feet 7 inches

*Vitall and Leopold Benguiat Collection, American Art Asso-
ciation, 1919*

360. RENAISSANCE CRIMSON VELVET REFECTORY TABLE
         RUNNER   *Genoese, XVI Century*
     Soft glowing velvet with rose tones and patina of age. Edged
     and cross-banded with gold galloon.

Length, 20 feet 3 inches; width, 1 foot 7 inches

361. GOLD- AND SILVER-EMBROIDERED GENOESE VELVET
         ARMORIAL BORDER   *Spanish or Italian, XVI Century*
     Finely preserved crimson velvet worked in gold and silver
     thread and colored silks, outlined in *cordonnets*, with a sym-
     metrical pattern of tall-stemmed vases of fruit emitting pairs
     of scrolling fuchsias, etc., and interrupted by three roun-
     dels charged with armorial bearings, one surmounted by a
     coronet.   *Length, 7 feet 6 inches; width, 10 inches*

362. ~~TWELVE~~ LENGTHS OF ROSE-CRIMSON SILK BROCATELLE
                              Louis Philippe Period
     Developing frames of rococo latticed scrollings centring
     naturalistic bouquets of roses, asters, and leafage. [Parts
     slightly worn.]

Total length, about 45½ yards; width, 1 foot 9 inches

363. JADE-GREEN SILK DAMASK HANGING

Italian, XVII Century

Aquamarine ground developing in a pale yellowish-green a figure composed of pairs of spreading leaves supporting a symmetrical floral trophy with two pendent curved and pointed leaves and short twigs bearing tiny pomegranates. Four widths. *Length, 8 feet 10 inches; width, 7 feet*

364. IMPORTANT RENAISSANCE CRIMSON VELVET HANGING

Genoese, XVI Century

Composed of three unusually long widths of fine old *cin-quecento* velvet with lustrous rose pile and heavily patinated with age; edged on three sides and banded in broad gold galloon. *Length, 18 feet 8 inches; width, 5 feet 5 inches*

365. IMPORTANT RENAISSANCE CRIMSON VELVET HANGING

Genoese, XVI Century

Similar to the preceding.

Length, 18 feet 8 inches; width, 5 feet 5 inches

TAPESTRIES

366. BRUSSELS TAPESTRY   *XVII Century*

THE SACRIFICE OF DIDO. A colorful scene, distinguished by the rich robes of the personages. On the right, before an altar of Jupiter and Diana, stands a priest in a blue robe, with a knife in his hand, over the body of a sacrificed lamb; about the foot of the altar are belaureled figures of acolytes bearing cressets and a dish to catch the blood of the animal.

[*Continued*]

124

366. *[Concluded]*

Before the altar, again, kneels Dido in sumptuous blue robes and crimson cloak, swinging a golden censer, while a white bull is led before her by a second priest to the sacrifice; behind them again are children, warriors, a Mongol holding a horse, and trumpeters. At either side of the composition, against a Vandyke brown ground, are female caryatids, one of them holding a goose, the other a censer, and an image of the golden calf; above and below scrolled cartouches with rich swags of flowers and fruit supported by flying cherubs above and by a swan and lamb below.

Height, 13 feet 6 inches; length, 15 feet 6 inches

[Illustrated as Frontispiece]

The following comprises a set of three important late Renaissance tapestries, THE STORY OF SAMSON, from the Brussels *atelier* of Jan Raes. This master is found at the beginning of the seventeenth century [1614] in Antwerp, and in collaboration with Jacob Geubels, Franz Sweerts and others engaged in the production of series, including *The Acts of the Apostles* and *The Story of Decius Mus;* he later appears in Brussels as a co-worker of the famous Van den Hecke. Raes was married to Margarete Van den Ackers, by whom he had three sons, Franz, Peter, and Jan, who carried on the fortunes of the family after his death, which occurred about 1635. His tapestries are usually found to bear his signature, together with workmen's monograms; the present series also bears the BB and shield mark of Brussels.

367. BRUSSELS RENAISSANCE TAPESTRY

By Jan Raes, circa 1620

SAMSON IS DENIED HIS WIFE [Judges XV, 1-5]. In the right foreground the giant in short brown robe and blue cloak, a kid under his arm, standing at the portal of his wife's dwelling in Timnath, her father and mother before the door refusing him admission; at a window of the palatial mansion, the woman is seen in the restraining grasp of a lover. In the right middle distance, Samson is portrayed setting fire in his rage to the Philistines' corn by loosing on it pairs of foxes with their tails tied together with a burning brand [*loc. cit.* v. 4, 5]. A magnificent border with ivory and rose-red grounds displays lusty figures of nude putti climbing upon rich bunches of fruit, flowers and foliage; at the four corners are circular medallions with Bacchic and leonine heads. At the centres of the sides are scrolled oval cartouches woven *en camaïeu* in yellow and Venetian-red, with the legends of ADAM AND EVE EXPELLED FROM PARADISE, JOSEPH AND POTIPHAR'S WIFE and the TOWER OF BABEL. In right-hand selvage workmen's monograms; at base, Brussels mark BB and shield.

Height, 13 *feet* 7 *inches; width,* 13 *feet* 1 *inch*

[Illustrated]

No. 367. Brussels Renaissance Tapestry

368. BRUSSELS RENAISSANCE TAPESTRY

By Jan Raes, circa 1620

SAMSON CARRIES AWAY THE GATES OF GAZA [Judges XVI, 1-3]. The powerful figure of Samson, in short red brocade tunic and flying blue cloak, the huge wooden gate borne on his shoulders, mounts in the foreground the hill towards Hebron; at the right are the Gazaite soldiers standing in fear and incredulity at the sight. In the middle distance appear the walls and classical cupolas of the city with the figures of the guards about the empty gate standing helpless as the hero bears them away. Border of the preceding, with slight variations; the cartouches depicting the SACRIFICES OF NOAH, THE BLIND ISAAC BLESSING JACOB and RAHAB AND THE ISRAELITE SPY. In right-hand selvage weaver's monogram; in base the signature of Jan Raes and Brussels mark BB and shield.

Height, 13 *feet* 9 *inches; length,* 17 *feet* 3 *inches*

[Illustrated]

Brussels Renaissance Ta

369. BRUSSELS RENAISSANCE TAPESTRY *By Jan Raes, circa* 1620

THE STORY OF SAMSON. At the left within a sumptuous interior with marble column is the figure of a woman, the wife of Menoah [?] in travail, surrounded by women attendants, two of whom are drying garments and bandages in the foreground; at the right appear two other Israelite women in blue robes bearing between them on a golden cloth a new-born child, probably symbolizing Samson. Before them stands the adult figure of the hero in red tunic and hose and green cloak, his hands raised in vigorous gesture, an elderly man standing beside him. Border of the preceding with slight variations; the cartouches display THE SACRIFICES OF NOAH, THE VISIT OF THE ANGEL TO ABRAHAM, RAHAB AND THE ISRAELITE SPY and THE BLIND ISAAC BLESSING JACOB. Lower selvage with Brussels mark BB and shield.

Height, 13 *feet* 8 *inches; length,* 20 *feet* 6 *inches*

[Illustrated]

No. 369. Brussels Renaissance Tapestry

The following comprises a series of four tapestries from the Paris *ateliers* of the period of Louis XIV and depicting THE STORY OF DIDO AND AENEAS; the vigorous and clear drawing and the delicacy of the borders should be remarked. They are of unusually practical size and as such greatly desirable.

370. PARIS TAPESTRY   *Late XVII Century*

AENEAS CARRYING AWAY ANCHISES FROM BURNING TROY. In the background appear the flaming walls of the city, with the great bridge, on which stands the wooden horse surrounded by soldiers. Striding away is the manly figure of Aeneas in blue tunic, cloak and plumed golden helmet, bearing on his back his father Anchises and attended at his right hand by his son Ascanius, who carries a boar spear and is clad in a yellow tunic and flying brown cloak. The procession moves towards a grove at the left in which is a temple with a shrine of the earth goddess Ceres. The unusual border, of tan shading into old-gold, is woven in blues, tans, yellow and ivory with festooned draperies interlacing with floral garlands, helmets, crossed swords and bows and quivers, and is centred at head and base with a drapery resting on quivers and arrows and supporting a crown, sceptre and necklace. In the upper corners are pairs of dolphin figures.

Height, 11 feet 2 inches; length, 12 feet

[Illustrated]

No. 370. Paris Tapestry

371. PARIS TAPESTRY   *Late XVII Century*

AENEAS DRIVEN BY A STORM INTO AFRICA. A confused multi-
tude of Greek warriors in boats and mastless vessels, is surg-
ing in from the right towards the shore before the gale; over-
head in the cloud-racked sky are flying geese, while in the
waves dolphins are sporting. On the stern of the vessel in
the foreground is a group of warriors over whom tower the
figures of Aeneas in his golden helmet and blue tunic and
his son Ascanius; at their feet is the old man Anchises, father
of Aeneas, childishly playing with dolls as the sailors struggle
to bring the craft to land. Border of the preceding.

Height, 11 feet 3 inches; length, 12 feet 9 inches

[Illustrated]

No. 371. Paris Tapestry

372. PARIS TAPESTRY *Late XVII Century*

THE BANQUET OF DIDO AND AENEAS. A rich marble interior hung with draperies and enriched with statues and shelves of golden vessels; at the left and above the portico are figures of musicians. Seated at the banquet table is the Tyrian king Belus and his queen; before them the hero Aeneas in blue tunic, salmon-pink cloak and golden helmet talking with Dido, who is accompanied by attendants, while behind Aeneas lounges the figure of his handsome son, the warrior Ascanius. Servants are bringing fruit and wine to the guests; on a chest at the right appears ominously the symbolical crown, sceptre and necklace which figure in the borders. Borders of the preceding.

Height, 11 *feet* 2 *inches; length,* 15 *feet* 8 *inches*

[Illustrated]

373. PARIS TAPESTRY   *Late XVII Century*

THE DEATH OF DIDO. Within a marble Corinthian chamber with niches bearing regal figures, is Dido, clad in a blue robe with brown and orange cloak and seated on a funeral pyre; a sword has pierced her breast, while around her flames are mounting from a mass of faggots, armor and vessels of wine, heaped together in disorder. In a doorway at the right is the agitated figure of a woman attendant who has arrived too late to save the abandoned queen. Borders of the preceding.

Height, 11 *feet* 5 *inches; width,* 9 *feet* 11 *inches*

[Illustrated]

374. EMERALD-GREEN SILK DAMASK HANGING

Spanish, Early XVIII Century

Design of small spatulate bouquets of blossoms enclosed between pairs of opposed curving leafy branches.

Length, 7 *feet* 6 *inches; width,* 8 *feet* 4 *inches*

From P. W. French and Company, New York

375. SET OF SPANISH LOUIS XIV CRIMSON SILK DAMASK ROOM HANGINGS

Comprising sixty-one pieces. Symmetrical design of ogival sprays of leaves and blossoms supporting large floral bouquets surmounted by pairs of pendent curved leaves and pomegranates interspersed with flowers. Variations in tone and color.

Total length, about 293 *yards* 30 *inches; widths from* 19½ *inches to* 21 *inches*

138

No. 373. Paris Tapestry

376. Rose-crimson Silk Brocatelle Hanging
Italian, XVII Century

Bold symmetrical design of huge spade-shaped sprays of leafage and fruit enclosed by ogivals of foliage and flowers supporting pairs of tiny Bérainesque canopies and fountains.

Total length, about 66½ yards; width, 24 inches

[Illustrated]

377. Important Rose-crimson Velvet Palace Hanging
Genoese, Early XVII Century

A remarkable piece composed of five widths of wonderfully preserved velvet of the Louis XIII period, with magnificent lustrous patina; bordered and cross-banded with gold galloon.

Length, 14 feet 4 inches; width, 9 feet 4 inches

378. Four Wine-red Velvet and Crimson Damask Curtains
Genoese, Early XVII Century

Heavy velvet with deep tones and thick pile; in beautiful preservation. Banded with gold galloon and fringe and finished at the head with crimson floral damask. Lined and interlined.

Length of each, 11 feet; width, 3 feet 6 inches

No. 376. Rose-crimson Silk Brocatelle Hanging

379. CRIMSON DAMASK FRIEZE FOR A SALON

Italian, XVII Century

Comprising eight pieces. Each composed of small panels of crimson damask with symmetrical foliage design separated by broad bands of gold galloon and trimmed with gold fringe. [One without fringe.]

Total length, about 55½ yards; depth, 13 inches

380. PAIR LOUIS XIV LEAF-GREEN AND GOLDEN-YELLOW BROCATELLE HANGINGS

Old-gold ground developing a brilliant symmetrical design of huge upstanding blossoms, foliage supported on festoons of leaves and enriched with blossoms. Trimmed with green and yellow silk ball fringe.

Length, 8 feet 4 inches; width, 4 feet 10 inches

381. TWO LOUIS XIV LEAF-GREEN AND GOLDEN-YELLOW BROCATELLE HANGINGS

Similar to the preceding.

Length of one, 9 feet 2 inches; width, 4 feet 10 inches
Length of one, 8 feet 8 inches; width, 4 feet 10 inches

[END OF SECOND AND LAST SESSION]

APPRAISALS FOR
UNITED STATES & STATE TAX
INSURANCE & OTHER PURPOSES
CATALOGUES OF PRIVATE
COLLECTIONS

THE American Art Association, Inc. will furnish appraisements, made by experts under its direct supervision, of art and literary property and all personal effects, in the settlement of estates, for inheritance tax, insurance and other purposes. ❦The Association is prepared to supplement this appraisal work by making catalogues of private libraries, of the contents of homes or of entire estates, such catalogues to be modeled after the fine and intelligently produced sales' catalogues of the Association. ❦Upon request the Association will furnish the names of many trust and insurance companies, executors, administrators, trustees, attorneys and private individuals for whom the Association has made appraisements which not only have been entirely satisfactory to them, but have been accepted by the United States Estate Tax Bureau, the State Tax Commission and others in interest.

AMERICAN ART ASSOCIATION · INC
Madison Avenue at 57th Street
NEW YORK

CPSIA information can be obtained
at www.ICGtesting.com
Printed in the USA
BVHW04s1129171018
530416BV00030B/2371/P

9 781528 204750